Everyday Heroes

Beth Johnson

TOWNSEND PRESS

Marlton, NJ 08053

Copyright © 1996, 2003 by Townsend Press, Inc.
Printed in the United States of America
ISBN 0-944210-26-0
9 8 7

**For book orders and requests for desk copies or supplements,
contact us in any of the following ways:**

By telephone: 1-800-772-6410
By fax: 1-800-225-8894
By e-mail: cs@townsendpress.com
Through our website: www.townsendpress.com

Copyright and Photo Acknowledgments

Ben Carson, M.D., with Cecil Murphey. Story on pages 167–172. From *Think Big*, copyright
© 1992 by Benjamin Carson, M.D. Reprinted by permission of Zondervan Publishing House.

Charles Cormany of San Rafael, California: Juan Angel, Yvonne Chavez, Gwendolyan Dasher,
Oscar de la Torre, Jackie Leno Grant, Juanita Lira, Enrique Rivas, and Kate Vant.

Paul Kowal of Cherry Hill, New Jersey: Maria Cardenas, Benjamin Carson on page 176,
Margaree Crosby, Joe Davis, Mikel Foster, Claire Henson, Rod Slappy, and Catina Washington.

Larry Marcus of Minneapolis, Minnesota: Grant Berry, Cindy Liu, and David McBeth.

Office of Communications and Public Affairs, Johns Hopkins Children's Center, Baltimore, Maryland:
Benjamin Carson on pages 167, 170, and 175.

Vince Rodriguez of Baltimore, Maryland: Benjamin Carson on the cover and on pages 169 and 173.

Susan Tusa of Detroit, Michigan: Kala White.

Design and Editorial Acknowledgments

Larry Didona designed the cover.

Janet Goldstein designed the book.

John Langan, Carole Mohr, and Judith Nadell edited the stories.

Note to Instructors

An Instructor's Manual and Answer Key is available for *Everyday Heroes*. Call our toll-free number
(1-800-772-6410), or contact us in any of the other ways listed above.

Contents

Introduction

Who Are "Everyday Heroes"?

Nowadays, when you ask people who their heroes are, they often can't think of anyone to name. They shake their heads and say, "It's sad. There are no real heroes anymore."

If they do come up with a name, it's usually of someone famous. The "hero" they choose might be someone they see on TV or on posters or in magazines. Film and music stars, TV celebrities, sports figures with multi-million-dollar contracts—these are frequently seen as the heroes of today.

Young people in particular get caught up in believing that a hero needs to be a rich, famous, larger-than-life figure. Certainly, it is natural enough to admire the talent of a popular entertainer or the skill of a great athlete, and it is hard not to be impressed by the money that such people make. But do success, riches, and fame really make a person a hero?

To answer that question, we need to define the word "hero." Is a hero simply someone who has achieved great financial and popular success? Is heroism just about money and fame? If so, any rich celebrity could qualify as a hero.

Or does being a hero have to do with the quality of a person's character? Is it more about courage, determination, and a kind of inner fire that keeps a person going in the face of all kinds of difficulties?

The men and women featured in this book are heroes of the second sort. With one exception, they are not famous. They are the kinds of people who might be your classmates, neighbors, friends, or relatives. Their lives have not been easy. They have faced obstacles that include poverty, racism, abuse, neglect, illness, drugs, and violence. Sometimes those obstacles have nearly destroyed their dreams. But each of them has found the strength to keep on going, to keep on trying. They have stood up to the challenges of life and said, "You will not defeat me. I will overcome." Such people are "everyday heroes."

Maybe you are experiencing some of the problems these men and women have faced. As you read these people's stories and as you talk and write about their lives, think about your own life. Can their stories teach you anything? Can they motivate you to deal with the obstacles that may stand in your path? Can they help you realize *your* potential to be an everyday hero?

To be a hero does not take money or fame. It does not take super-human athletic ability or a Grammy-award-winning voice. As you will see in these stories, what it takes is the determination to work hard and pursue dreams no matter what stands in the way. That's the most exciting challenge that any of us can face.

How to Use This Book

The purpose of this book is to inspire you to do your best—and to help you develop important reading, thinking, and writing skills. The skills will deepen your appreciation of the stories. They can also make you more successful in school and at work.

Before each story are a **preview** and and a **word list**. Then comes the story. Some stories are *written by* the person. For example, one story begins, "When I was a kid in Nevada, Missouri, I suffered from a speech disorder." Other stories are *written about* the person. For instance, another story begins, "In a rare moment of rest in the living room of his crowded trailer home, Juan Angel smiles as he watches his children play."

Each story includes photographs so that you will get an even better sense of the person in question. The photographs show that person going about daily routines at work, at school, at home, and with special people in his or her life. Given the fact that each person has been through difficult times, it is inspiring to see so many smiles in the photos and to have such strong visual evidence that, "Yes, this person has made it."

Each story is followed by **vocabulary**, **reading**, and **discussion questions** as well as **writing assignments**. Starting on the next page is a brief version of the kind of story that appears in the book, along with sample activities and explanatory notes. Reading the story and going through the notes and activities will give you a good idea of how *Everyday Heroes* works.

A Sample Story

A childhood illness left Elda Sara Morgan with a frightening medical condition. Her health problems made it unlikely that she would have many friends, do well in school, or pursue a satisfying career. Yet today she has accomplished all this and more. Her story shows what can happen when a person is determined to succeed.

➤ *Note:* The preview that introduces each story is set off in a shaded box. Read it to get a quick idea of what the story is about.

Elda Sara Morgan

Words to Watch

thrashing (4): moving wildly
The turtle lay on its back, its legs *thrashing* as it tried to turn over.

implied (8): suggested without saying directly
The teacher's expression *implied* that she did not believe my excuse for being late.

➤ *Note:* "Words to Watch" is a list of some of the more difficult words in the story and their meanings. The numbers in parentheses refer to the paragraphs in the story where the words first appear. For example, *thrashing* is in paragraph 4 of the story. A sentence is then given using each word to help you better understand its meaning. Each of the "Words to Watch" is marked in the story by a small raised circle (°).

1 When I was two years old, I caught the German measles. I got over the measles, but my high fever at the time led to another problem. I developed the disorder called epilepsy.

2 In a normal brain, nerve cells constantly fire off tiny electrical signals that tell the body what to do. When a person has epilepsy, those signals go wild. Instead of sending small, controlled signals, the nerve cells produce wild electrical storms of activity.

3 When one of those epileptic storms went off in my brain, I would have an attack known as a seizure. If it was a small seizure, I would simply lose track of what was happening around me for a few seconds. For example, if my teacher was saying, "The farmer gave the horses some hay," I might hear only, "The farmer hay." To people around me, it would look as though I had spaced out for a few seconds.

4 A major seizure was very different and was frightening to watch. I would fall to the floor, my face turning blue from lack of oxygen. My body would shake violently, with my arms and legs thrashing° in strange positions. My family knew that the seizure would soon pass and that all they could do was put something in my mouth, like a spoon, to keep me from choking on

my tongue. When a seizure happened in the classroom, another student would run to get my older sister to help me.

5 I was fortunate to have a family who loved me and parents who saw me as more than just an epileptic. To my parents I was always Elda Sara, their daughter, and I was able to achieve anything I put my mind to. "You're only disabled if you choose to be," my father would say. "Never say 'I can't.' There is no such thing as 'can't' in this house."

6 My family's attitude helped me fight the limitations of epilepsy. Unfortunately, the rest of my world was less supportive. Many students, and even some teachers, were afraid of me. I was "accidentally" pushed down a flight of stairs on one occasion. Students tripped me, pushed me, and knocked books out of my hands. One teacher called me a "stupid retard" in front of the other students. I still remember how my heart hurt when she said those words.

7 My seizures stopped when I was 13 years old and in seventh grade. But many students still continued to ignore me or be mean to me. My way of reacting to other students' abuse was to withdraw into my schoolwork. I became an outstanding student, especially in the sciences. In fact, my science teacher, Mr. Thomas Fisher, asked me to tutor some of my classmates in biology. I was only a sophomore, and some of the people I was tutoring were seniors. I became friends with some of the students I tutored. That, and a lot of compliments from Mr. Fisher, gave my self-confidence a real boost. Finally, school began to be a place that I liked to be.

8 I started thinking about becoming a science teacher or a nurse. However, my guidance counselor told me that epileptics couldn't do those things. He continu-ally discouraged me from taking advanced science classes. He implied° that, despite my straight A's, I was not smart enough to succeed in them.

9 I'll never forget my last visit to this guidance counselor. When I finished high school, I was on the honor roll and had earned many more credits than I needed to graduate. I went into his office and showed him my report card and transcript. "I made it through high school, without too much help from you," I told him. "You decided a long time ago that I couldn't ever amount to anything. I think I've proved you wrong. And you haven't heard the last of me yet." He just stared at me, open-mouthed. But another counselor who heard me started applauding. I left the office feeling pretty great.

10 I'm in my senior year now at American International College in Springfield, Massachusetts, preparing to be a special-education teacher. I'm doing student teaching in a first-grade class. I think of my twenty-eight students as flowers in a garden, each of them different, but each of them precious and beautiful and needing my help to blossom.

11 While my seizures have stopped, my health problems have not. Some days I have to deal with severe pain in my legs that makes it hard to walk. Sometimes I have muscle weakness which affects the strength in my hands. The doctors say that within ten years I may not be able to walk or hold anything.

12 But maybe the doctors are wrong. Or maybe there will be a medical breakthrough that will help me. Even if I do lose the use of my hands and legs, I know that I'll deal with it. I teach Bible study classes to a group of inner-city girls. I tell them, "No, life isn't a bed of roses. But there are paths out of the thorns and into places of great beauty."

➤ *Note:* Now that you have read the story, work through the sample vocabulary and reading questions that follow. Then think about the discussion question and look at the suggested answer. Finally, read the writing assignment and one student's response.

Vocabulary Check

➤ *Note:* There are five "Vocabulary Check" questions for each reading. The opening questions give practice in two or more of the "Words to Watch" that appear before the story. In the question below, use the "Words to Watch" definition on page 3 for *thrashing* to figure out which sentence would make sense with the word. Circle the letter of your answer.

1. In which sentence would the word **thrashing** make sense?
   a. My cousin got a ticket for driving through a _____ red light.
   b. On a calm day like this, it is pleasant to hear the waves _____ gently on the beach.
   c. The children's _____ in the bathtub left the floor soaking wet.

   Explanation:

   To answer this question, you had to either remember or check the meaning of *thrashing* in "Words to Watch." There you are told that *thrashing* means "moving wildly." The only sentence in the question in which that meaning fits is *c*: The children's thrashing *[moving wildly]* in the bathtub left the floor soaking wet.

➤ *Note:* The closing "Vocabulary Check" questions give you practice in figuring out the meaning of a word by looking at its **context**—the other words in the sentence. Figure out from the context what *severe* means in the sentence below, and circle the letter of your answer.

2. In the sentence below, the word **severe** means
   a. extreme.
   b. helpful.
   c. noisy.

   "Some days I have to deal with severe pain in my legs that makes it hard to walk." (Paragraph 11)

   Explanation:

   To answer this question, you had to look at the context of the word *severe*. That context suggests that the pain is so extreme that Elda Sara has trouble walking. So the answer to question 2 is *a*.

Reading Check

➤ *Note:* Each "Reading Check" contains ten reading-skill questions. The questions deal with the central point, main ideas, supporting details, and conclusions.

Central Point

➤ *Note:* The **central point** is what the whole reading is about. It is the main idea of the entire story. To find it, ask yourself, "Which statement best summarizes the entire story?"

There is one central-point question for each story. Circle the letter of your answer for the central-point question below.

1. What is the central point of this reading?
    a. Elda Sara had a disorder called epilepsy that caused her to have minor and major seizures.
    b. Some students and teachers in her school were cruel to Elda Sara.
    c. With the help of her parents and a teacher, Elda Sara rose above the problems of epilepsy.

    ### *Explanation:*
    • The information in answer *a* is accurate, but it is too limited to be the central point. The story tells us much more than the fact that Elda Sara had epilepsy. Remember that the central point must cover the *entire* reading.
    • The information in answer *b* is accurate as well. But it tells us only about the negative attitudes towards Elda Sara. It does not cover other parts of the reading, such as Elda Sara's success.
    • Only answer *c* gives the central point of the reading: Elda Sara, with the help of others, has been able to rise above the problems of epilepsy.

Main Ideas

➤ *Note:* The **main idea** is the chief point of the paragraph. Everything, or almost everything, in the paragraph is about that one point. To find the main idea, ask yourself, "Which statement best summarizes the entire paragraph?"

There are usually three main-idea questions for each story. Circle the letter of your answer for the main-idea question below.

2. What is the main idea of paragraph 8?
    a. Elda Sara wanted to become a science teacher or a nurse.
    b. Elda Sara earned straight A's in her science courses.
    c. The guidance counselor discouraged Elda Sara from aiming for her career choices despite her good grades.

Explanation:

- The information in answers *a* and *b* is true, but each answer is too limited to be the main idea. Neither mentions the key point about Elda Sara's guidance counselor. Remember, the main idea should summarize all or most of the paragraph.
- Only answer *c* summarizes the whole paragraph: The counselor discouraged Elda Sara from pursuing teaching or nursing despite her good grades.

Supporting Details

➤ *Note:* **Supporting details** explain or develop the central point and main ideas of a story. To find key supporting details, you must read a story carefully.

There are usually three supporting-detail questions for each story. Circle the letter of your answer for the supporting-detail question below.

3. When Elda Sara was a sophomore in high school, her science teacher asked her to
    a. drop out of biology.
    b. give a talk on epilepsy to the class.
    c. tutor other students in biology.

Explanation:

- Answers *a* and *b* are nowhere in the story.
- The correct answer, *c*, can be found in paragraph 7 of the story.

Conclusions

➤ *Note:* A **conclusion** is an idea that is not stated directly but that is hinted at or suggested. You draw conclusions in everyday life all the time. For example, let's say you are looking for your new English class, and you walk into a room full of musical instruments. You will quickly conclude that you are in the wrong room. You can draw conclusions about what you read in the same way. Using your own experience and common sense, you can think about what is suggested indirectly in a reading.

There are usually three conclusion questions for each story. Circle the letter of your answer for the conclusion question below.

4. You can conclude from paragraph 9 that
    a. the guidance counselor was not at all surprised that Elda Sara spoke to him so strongly.
    b. Elda Sara found it satisfying to show the guidance counselor that he had been wrong about her.
    c. Elda Sara had always been an extremely shy person.

Explanation:

- Answer *a* could not be correct. The guidance counselor was "open-mouthed," which tells us he was surprised by Elda Sara's words.

- Answer *c* is also incorrect. A very shy person would not be likely to march into the counselor's office and tell him forcefully that he had been wrong.

- Only answer *b* can be right. Elda Sara's comment that she felt "pretty great" as she left the office tells us that she found the experience satisfying.

Questions for Thinking and Discussion

➤ *Note:* These questions help you to think about ideas raised by the story and to make connections between the story and your own life. Each reading includes three of these questions. Take several minutes to think and talk about the question below.

1. Elda Sara said that most students reacted to her epilepsy by either ignoring her or being cruel to her. Have you ever seen people reacting this way to someone with a disability? Why, in your opinion, do people at times respond cruelly to someone who is "different"?

   ### Explanation:

   Answers to this question will vary, of course. Probably all of us can tell a story about someone who seemed different in some way, and how other people responded. Perhaps people pick on a disabled person out of fear. Maybe they are afraid that the disability will somehow "rub off" on them. Maybe they are afraid that if they are nice to the disabled person, they will be picked on too. Maybe if they put down another person, they make themselves feel a little more important.

Ideas for Writing

➤ *Note:* After each story in the book, there are two writing assignments. The assignments give you a chance to explore further some of the interesting ideas in the story. They also help you look more closely at what you value, whom you respect, and how you react to people and situations.

   On the next page are a writing assignment and a sample paper written in response to the assignment. After you read the paper, read the explanation that follows. The explanation first discusses the sample paper. Then it tells about some methods you can use when writing your own papers.

1. Elda Sara's attitudes suggest that she will become a good teacher. What qualities do you feel make a teacher good? Think about a teacher you liked and respected. Then write a paper explaining a few qualities that made him or her such a fine teacher. Give examples from your own experience that show why he or she was so good.

A Sample Paper:

A Good Teacher

My third-grade teacher, Mrs. Latimore, was one of the best teachers I have ever known. For one thing, she had a sense of humor. When she read stories out loud, she got us to laugh by making up funny voices for the characters in the story. Sometimes when a student would go up to her desk for help, she'd say, "What's up, Doc?" like Bugs Bunny. Mrs. Latimore was also patient. If students had trouble understanding a math problem or a grammar point, she would take the time needed to explain it again. If we were a little noisy at the start of a class, she waited a couple of minutes for us to calm down. Finally, Mrs. Latimore was a kind person. She was always saying positive things, like "Martha really likes to help other people" or "Edward has a lot of musical talent." Whenever someone had a birthday, she would announce it, and the class would sing "Happy Birthday" to that person and then applaud. Even years later, other students and I still talked about how much we enjoyed Mrs. Latimore as a teacher.

Explanation:

The above paper is an effective one. It begins by making a clear point—that Mrs. Latimore was a good teacher. It then supports that point by naming three qualities that made her a good teacher—a sense of humor, patience, and kindness. We are given examples of each of those qualities. The examples show how Mrs. Latimore behaved, what she said, and how she reacted. The details let us see clearly for ourselves that Mrs. Latimore was a good teacher. The writer has truly supplied the evidence needed to back up her opening point.

When writing a paper, it is often a good idea to make your main point near the beginning. Then develop that point with plenty of supporting details.

You can often find your main point and supporting details by using one or more useful methods. One is simply to *write down without stopping* as many ideas about your topic as you can think of. Don't worry yet about spelling or punctuation or grammar. Just get your thoughts down on paper. Doing this kind of "freewriting" for a while will help you decide on a point for your paper. It will also provide you with ideas for supporting details.

Another way to think about your paper is to *make lists*. For instance, to prepare for the above paper, the writer could have written the names of two or three of her favorite teachers. She could then have listed the qualities that made each one so good and some examples of those qualities. At some point she could have selected the teacher that seemed like the best subject for the paper.

A third approach is to *ask yourself questions* about your topic. Writing down your questions and answers will give you a good start on a paper. For instance, the writer of the paper about Mrs. Latimore could have asked herself such questions as, "Why was she popular? What did she do that I liked? What did she say? When was she helpful to me?"

Writing down your thoughts, making lists, asking yourself questions—all these methods can help you get started when it comes time to write a paper.

A Final Word

By now you have a sense of *Everyday Heroes* and how it is organized. You have learned about the stories and the activities that follow them. The activities can help you become a stronger reader, thinker, and writer. But they are not the most important part of the book. The twenty stories are. Read and enjoy the stories. Get to know the people they describe. Study the photographs. Experience the feelings that the stories call up in you—anger, sympathy, respect, sadness, amusement, triumph. Travel for a while in the worlds of these everyday heroes. The only passport you need is the willingness to read, to learn, and to grow. *Everyday Heroes* is a book to explore with your mind, but even more than that, with your heart.

Rod Slappy was "the suspension king"—a kid with such a behavior problem that his home school district washed its hands of him. Today he runs an exciting educational program that has drawn praise from the governor of his state. His story proves that he's a "big man" in more ways than one.

1 / Rod Slappy

Words to Watch

dismayed (6): troubled; alarmed
Farmers were *dismayed* by the lack of rain for their crops.

urban (8): located in a city
The Fresh Air program gives *urban* children a taste of country life.

focus (14): concentrate
I can't *focus* on my reading while that music is playing.

romanticized (15): viewed in too positive a way
The boy *romanticized* quitting school. He thought it meant freedom.

daze (23): a confused state
The news showed earthquake survivors wandering around in a *daze*.

Rod Slappy works with two students in his class.

Rod Slappy, a junior-high-school student, is on his way from art class to shop. At age 13, he is six feet one inch tall. He weighs 190 pounds. Rod's attitude is as scary as his size. He enjoys the impression he makes as he walks down the hall. He wants to see fear in other students' eyes. He wants to see them moving out of his way or approaching him with respect.

A girl named Charlene Hill speaks to Rod. She likes him, that is clear. He kind of likes her, too. He often teases her about her long, skinny arms and legs. His nickname for her is "Spider." He calls her that now. She answers back with her own teasing insult. Rod's voice rises. Charlene is not supposed to speak to him like that, but she keeps coming back. Her voice grows louder, too. Soon the two are shouting at one another. Their cursing fills the halls of the school. Other students gather around to watch and listen.

A man pushes his way through the crowd. It is Mr. Turner, a social studies teacher. He knows Rod, of course. All the teachers at Myrtle Avenue Junior High know Rod. When a student has been suspended from elementary school fifty-two times, as Rod has, teachers generally hear about it. But Mr. Turner has always been on pretty good terms with Rod. He seems to see a spark of promise in the young boy. Mr. Turner lays a hand on

Rod's arm. He politely suggests that Rod move on to shop class.

4   If Rod, Charlene, and Mr. Turner were the only people around, Rod might do as Mr. Turner asked. But there is a crowd watching. Rod doesn't want anyone to say he let a teacher disrespect him. Rod turns on Mr. Turner and pushes him hard. The teacher stumbles into the crowd of students. Then he comes back at Rod. Mr. Turner is a strong man. He grabs Rod's collar and begins to pull him towards the principal's office. Rod breaks away and pushes Mr. Turner again. The fight goes on for several minutes. Finally a security guard arrives and helps Mr. Turner get control of Rod.

5   Later that day, Rod is sitting in the superintendent's office. His mother is there, too. She has been called away from her job. A folder lies on the desk before them. It contains dozens of papers. The papers report Rod's supensions from school. They tell of his fights with other students. Now a new paper lies on top of the folder. It describes Rod's attack on a teacher. The superintendent is speaking to Rod's mother. "We will not accept Rod in this school district ever again," he tells her. "You'll have to find another school willing to take him."

6   Rod looks at his mother's face. He is dismayed° by what he sees. He has been in trouble many times in the past. But until today, he has known that she believed in him. She always had hope that he would do better. But today her face is hopeless. She cannot ask that Rod be given another chance. Not with that overflowing folder lying there for everyone to see. All she can do is drop her head and cry. She has to accept the fact that her son may be lost.

7   Fourteen years later, a reporter from the *Philadelphia Inquirer* is visiting an unusual fifth-grade classroom in Camden, New Jersey. There are thirty-one students there. All are boys. All have had a hard time in school in the past. Some have failed many of their classes. Others are always getting into fights. Some skip school frequently.

8   These boys are students in a program called the Urban° Males class. They study reading and arithmetic, like other fifth graders. But they talk about many other things, too. They talk about Malcolm X and Snoop Doggy Dogg. They learn about family planning and how to choose healthy foods. They talk about what a man owes to his wife, his children, and his community. They learn, as the *Inquirer* reporter writes, "that street smarts don't have to cancel out school smarts."

9   The program works. The *Inquirer* article says, "After just five months in class, the boys no longer scrap during recess or squabble during lessons. They sit up tall and straight in their chairs. They dress smartly in uniforms of blue pants, white shirts, and ties. . . . And they daily recite the Urban Male Oath from memory, shouting the words proudly:

> *'The responsibilities of a man are:*
> *God! God without man is still God,*
> *   but man without God is nothing.*
> *Family! A spiritual man makes a*
> *   family complete.*
> *Education! Knowledge is power.*
> *Job! A man who doesn't work should*
> *   not eat.*
> *Nutrition! The body is a temple.*
> *Exercise! Exercise cleanses the mind.'"*

10   One of the Urban Males students, Justin Coleman, reports on what he's learned from the class. "If we get into a fight somewhere, we learn how to just walk away. To be a man, you don't have to fight and go around with different girls."

11   Khadijah Muhammad has two sons in the class, Benny and Talib. She says, "Our children, a lot of them are lost.

There are 11- and 12-year-olds selling drugs on corners. We need more programs like this. We need more teachers like Mr. Slappy."

12   She said "Mr. Slappy." In fact, it's the same Rod Slappy who, fourteen years before, spent more time in detention hall than in class. It's the same Rod Slappy who was in more than a hundred fights in elementary school and who was told by his home school district, "Go away and never come back." Now Rod Slappy is back in school, standing in front of thirty-one boys. And these days, he's dressed in a dark suit, white shirt, and tie. He's a graduate of a high-class Pennsylvania college. His ideas about education have been praised by the governor of New Jersey. He's married now. He and his wife are saving money, building a home together, hoping to start a family somewhere down the road.

What happened to Rod Slappy in the past fourteen years? How could he have changed so much?   13

Much of the credit belongs to Rod himself. Even when he was in constant trouble, he had many good qualities. He was born with plenty of intelligence, charm, and ability. "I was always a focused kid," he says today. "The question was, what would I focus° on?"   14

Until he was kicked out of junior high, Rod's main interest was clear. He wanted to be impressive on the street. His hero was a neighborhood man named Lonnie. "Lonnie represented what I wanted at that time," Rod says. "He had lots of girls. Lots of gold. Flashy cars. I romanticized° him. I wanted that career path. I wanted to walk down the street and hear people say, 'Don't mess with him.'"   15

But even then, Rod was attracted to another example. That was Lonnie's brother, Mark. Mark was a lawyer. "Mark was the complete opposite of Lonnie," Rod says. "He had a good job. He had a home in the suburbs. My mother was in love with Mark and all he stood for." Rod remembers how Mark would come visit the neighborhood. "He'd ease over to speak to me, ask what I was up to. There was a tug-of-war between those two images in my mind. Mark had the suit, the home, the family, the job. Lonnie had all that flash."   16

Today, Lonnie is doing prison time for rape. Rod still sees Mark from time to time. "Mark tells me he is proud of me. He didn't think I was listening to what he had to say."   17

Rod says Mark was part of "a chain of caring adults. They were people who pulled me along. They tried to help me handle the twists and turns of life." There were such adults in Rod's life before his fight with Mr. Turner. They were like the teacher who once told him, "Rod, if you ever get your head screwed on right, you are going to set fire to this world."   18

19   But after being expelled from junior high, Rod thought that chain had reached its end. Who would ever believe in him again?

20   The answer to Rod's question was found in St. Benedict's School. It was an all-boys school run by a group of monks in Newark, New Jersey. The school agreed to take Rod in for a trial period. If he did well during the summer, he could stay.

21   Rod was relieved to be accepted at St. Benedict's. However, as he says today, "old ways are hard to change." He behaved well at the school for two weeks. Then he began to tease another student. His name was Luis, but the boys called him "Panama" because he came from that country. One afternoon, when the English teacher was out of the room, Rod called Panama "a punk." Panama argued with Rod. Rod kicked Panama in the stomach. Panama picked up a chair and threw it at Rod. Rod threw it back. Several windows were soon shattered by the flying chair. By the time a teacher ran in and stopped the fight, the floor was covered with broken glass. Rod was sent to the headmaster's office.

22   Rod sat in the office. He knew he'd ruined his chance to stay at St. Benedict's. He knew he had destroyed his mother's final hope. He stared at the floor until he heard the swish of a monk's robes beside him. He looked at the face of the headmaster, Father Edwin Leahy. He then glanced nervously away. He stole another look. Slowly he realized that Father Edwin was not looking at him with disgust. He didn't even look angry. Instead, his eyes shone with hope and patience. He spoke gently to Rod. "You are an intelligent young man," he said. "Don't fight anymore. Go upstairs and sweep up that glass. Then get back to class."

23   In a daze°, Rod took the broom and dustpan Father Edwin was holding out to him. Finally he asked, "Aren't you going to suspend me? Aren't you going to tell me I'll never amount to anything?" Father Edwin shook his head. "No," he answered. "I don't believe in children missing school. You're going to be something great someday. Now go sweep up that glass."

Rod plays football after school with his students.

24   Father Edwin never mentioned the fight again. "When he'd see me in the hall, he'd just say, 'Hi, Rod. How are you doing?'" Rod remembers. "If he saw me working in class, he'd lay his hand on my shoulder and say, 'You're going to do fine.'"

25   Rod realized what Father Edwin was telling him. The headmaster was making Rod an offer. He would gladly forget about Rod's past forever if Rod wanted to change. That offer impressed Rod. He decided he would not let Father Edwin down. He completed the summer term with two B's and two C's. Four years later he graduated from St. Benedict's with a B+ average. He had earned a varsity

letter in basketball and done well on his college entrance tests. He was accepted by some of the best colleges in the country. He chose to attend Franklin and Marshall College in Lancaster, Pennsylvania.

26   At Franklin and Marshall, Rod faced new struggles. He was competing against students from wealthy, well-educated families. Sometimes it was difficult to keep up. Not everyone at the college was encouraging. "I had one professor say to me, 'What are you doing here? You don't belong in this school,'" Rod said. Rod is an African-American, and Franklin and Marshall is a largely white school. But he says, "I think that kind of reaction was less a racial thing than a class thing. It was like they were saying, 'You're from Newark. You're from the projects. You don't fit in.'"

27   At the same time, Rod was discovering that he loved sociology. "I had a knack for it. I was a good observer of human behavior," he says. His sociology professors encouraged him. "They pushed me hard," Rod remembers. "They talked to me as if I was a Harvard professor. They saw that my writing skills weren't sharp, and they made me realize I had to do better. My papers would come back again and again and again. But through it all, they believed in me. They made me realize, *I can do this*. I can succeed in this world."

28   One of Rod's sociology professors was Katherine McClelland. She helped him develop the idea for the Urban Males class he teaches today. Rod had been working in a management training program with AT&T. "I was making lots of money, but I was bored to tears," he says. Professor McClelland asked him, "What do you really want to do?" Rod told her, "I want to work with kids who are like I was." She told him, "Go do it." She began sending him articles about city kids and their needs. Rod put together a proposal for the Urban Males program. The Camden City School District accepted it.

29   As Rod now moves through his Camden classroom, he feels those thirty-one pairs of eyes upon him. He is aware of the responsibility he carries. He remembers what it's like to be an inner-city boy whose father isn't around. "I loved my mom, but at a certain age a boy wants his father," Rod says, his eyes sad with the memories. "I was really angry that he wasn't around. I was angrier still when he died. There was so much I wanted to know from my dad. I wanted to see how his hair grew because that's what my hair would be like some day. I wanted to see his hands because that's what my hands would look like. I wanted to watch him walk to see if my strides could match his. I wanted to know what I would be like, and I thought only he could show me."

30   Today, Rod provides such glimpses into the future for his thirty-one boys. It's part of his job. "I feel them studying me," he says. "They watch how I stand, how I dress, how I speak. That's the best part of my job. I'm helping raise them, in a sense."

31   "I talk to them about everything," Rod continues. "I tell them, for instance, about going back to the neighborhood. My old friends laugh at me about not having a child yet. They don't support my wife and me in our plans to wait until we're ready. Instead, they say, 'What's the matter with you? You can't make a baby?' And I admit, that bothers me. I don't like to hear it. But it doesn't change who I am or what I think is right.

32   "I tell my students that's what life is," Rod says. "It's about struggles. It's about problems. It's about failing, but trying again. I say, 'Let's talk about this. Let's write about this.' And before you know it," he says, a grin creasing his broad face, "you've got them working fractions."

Vocabulary Check

1. In which sentence does the word **urban** make sense?
   a. Her grades were very high, so she was admitted to an _____ class.
   b. One of the pleasures of _____ life is the street vendors selling all kinds of food.
   c. This chili was so _____ it made my mouth burn for hours after I ate it.

2. In which sentence does the word **daze** make sense?
   a. My neighbor was in a happy _____ after learning she'd won a new car.
   b. Everyone agrees that the artwork shows a lot of _____.
   c. Once a year, the fifth graders have five _____ of achievement tests.

3. In the sentences below, the word **trial** means
   a. expensive.
   b. permanent.
   c. test.

   "The school agreed to take Rod in for a trial period. If he did well during the summer, he could stay." (Paragraph 20)

Rod relaxes at home with his wife, Jean.

4. In the sentence below, the word **relieved** means
   a. comforted.
   b. annoyed.
   c. sorry.

   "Rod was relieved to be accepted at St. Benedict's." (Paragraph 21)

5. In the sentences below, the word **proposal** means
   a. an offer of marriage.
   b. a bill.
   c. a suggested plan.

   "Rod put together a proposal for the Urban Males program. The Camden City School District accepted it." (Paragraph 28)

SCORE: **(Number correct)** _____ **x 20 =** _____%

Reading Check

Central Point and Main Ideas

1. What is the central point of the reading?
   a. Father Leahy's patient trust was a great encouragement to Rod.
   b. With help from others, Rod chose a moral, useful life over a violent and irresponsible one.
   c. Despite numerous school fights and suspensions, Rod managed to graduate from a special high school.

2. What is the main idea of paragraph 6?
   a. The attack on a teacher made even Rod's mother lose hope for Rod.
   b. Rod's mother hopes that Rod will eventually do better in school.
   c. The folder on the superintendent's desk was filled with complaints about Rod.

3. What is the main idea of paragraph 12?
   a. Rod is now the teacher of a class of thirty-one boys.
   b. Rod and his wife are hoping to start a family in a few years.
   c. There is a big difference between Rod Slappy's past and present.

4. What is the main idea of paragraph 25?
   a. Rod graduated from St. Benedict's School with a B+ average and a varsity letter in basketball.
   b. Because of Father Edwin's encouragement, Rod became a good student and went on to a good college.
   c. Father Edwin was willing to forget about Rod's past.

Supporting Details

5. The two brothers whose examples attracted Rod were
   a. a lawyer and a criminal.
   b. a fighter and a monk.
   c. a teacher and a lawyer.

6. Rod was finally expelled from junior high for
   a. using drugs.
   b. skipping school.
   c. attacking a teacher.

7. The Urban Males program was designed by
   a. Father Edwin Leahy, the headmaster at St. Benedict's School.
   b. Rod Slappy.
   c. Franklin and Marshall College.

Conclusions

8. You can conclude from paragraph 2 that
   a. in junior high, Rod always gave nicknames to people he knew.
   b. Rod's tough image was more important to him than friendship with Charlene.
   c. as the shouting match grew louder, Rod began to hit Charlene.

9. You can conclude from paragraph 25 that
   a. most of the students at St. Benedict's School went on to college.
   b. it is possible for someone to greatly change the direction of his or her life.
   c. it was easy to get good grades at St. Benedict's.

10. You can conclude from paragraph 29 that
    a. Rod's father was often angry with him.
    b. Rod's father was rarely around when Rod was growing up.
    c. Rod knows his father very well.

SCORE: (Number correct) _____ x 10 = _____%

Questions for Thinking and Discussion

1. What do you think of the Urban Males class that Rod Slappy has created?

2. As a child, Rod was torn between the opposing examples set by two brothers who lived in his neighborhood. Do you know two people who have sharply different lifestyles? Describe the different choices they have made.

3. Father Edwin was not the first adult to treat Rod kindly or encourage him to succeed. Why do you think he influenced Rod in a way that no other adult had previously?

Rod discusses a point in class with his students.

Rod helps one of his students write a story.

Ideas for Writing

1. Pretend that you are Mark, the man from Rod's neighborhood who became a lawyer. Imagine that you hear about 12-year-old Rod, who is constantly getting into trouble at school and hanging out in the street. As Mark, write Rod a letter in which you try to convince him to change his ways.

2. What adults have been a good influence on your life? Write a paper describing a specific time that one of those adults made you feel special.

2 / Yvonne Chavez

Yvonne Chavez was a teenage mother with gang involvement in her past and with an abusive marriage in her present. By the age of 17, she believed that she had nothing to look forward to. But when she found the strength to demand that others respect her, she discovered a rewarding life still lay ahead.

Words to Watch

inconsolably (5): in a way that makes comforting impossible
My niece was *inconsolably* sad when her kitten died.

haven (6): a protected, sheltered place
For a few dozen homeless people, the church shelter was a *haven* from the cold rain.

devastated (8): shocked and hurt
My aunt was *devastated* when she was accused of stealing.

deteriorate (17): become worse
During the long dry spell, the garden began to *deteriorate*.

tolerate (22): put up with; permit
That teacher will not *tolerate* bad manners.

Yvonne Chavez sits reading on campus.

When I was a little girl, I wondered if I were the only child who didn't have a father. I found my birth certificate and asked my mother why the line that asked for "father's name" had been left blank. She brushed me off, saying, "Oh, put that away and stop asking so many questions."

But I didn't stop. I kept asking who my father was and, more importantly, when I could see him. Finally, tired out, my mother answered, "Your father's at work like all the other family men. Go to sleep, and he'll be back tomorrow." I was so happy and excited that I barely slept that night. I wanted to be awake and ready when he arrived.

The next day I rushed from my bed, anxiously asking my mother, *"Mami, ya está aquí mi papá?* Is he here yet, Mommy?"

"Ay niña, como das lata con lo mismo. You're getting on my nerves, little girl. Your father is never coming back. He left when I was pregnant because he didn't want you!"

The words my mother shouted at me that morning still ring in my ears. I cried inconsolably° all day. Never again was the subject of my father brought up. To this day, I don't even know his name.

Because my mother and I were alone together, she meant everything to me. I believed she would always provide me with security and comfort. But one day, I learned that I could not depend on that safe haven°.

7   My mother had a woman friend who attended our church with her husband. We went to their house for a visit. I was five years old. While the two women sat talking over coffee at the kitchen table, the man said he needed to get something from the garage. He asked me to go with him. Once we were in the garage, he molested me. I was too frightened and confused to say anything when we returned to the house. But once my mother and I were alone, I told her what had happened. I thought she would make the shame I felt inside go away. However, she did nothing. She told me that God would take care of the man who had hurt me. She said that no one wanted to hear about what had happened and that I should forget about it.

8   I was devastated°. I wanted my mother—not God—to take care of the situation. For the first time in my life, I felt I had no one to turn to for protection.

9   Elementary school was an unhappy experience for me. I was constantly teased by other children because I was overweight and illegitimate. But then junior high came along, and I entered a different world. For the first time I was exposed to drugs, parties, sex, and gangs.

10   A lot of people don't understand about gangs. They read things in the paper, shake their heads and say, "How can a kid end up in jail at age 14?" I admire the people who resist getting involved in gangs. But that's hard to do when you grow up in a neighborhood where gangs are all there is. Crackheads and gangsters are the only people you have to look up to.

11   For me, the gang provided an easy solution to all my problems. I wanted to belong to a crowd. I wanted to be someone others would look up to. My gang, Diamond Street, provided all that. My schoolmates respected me. Everyone wanted to be my friend. It thrilled me to hear people call out my *placaso*, my gang name: "Hey, Smiley!" Although my drug use and fights with other women caused me pain, I thought that the love and respect I received from my new *familia* made it all worthwhile.

12   Soon after I joined the gang, I met Samuel. Samuel had grown up in South Central Los Angeles, the toughest section of the city, with his mother and five brothers and sisters. He was taken into the gang when he was 12. I was in love with him, or at least I thought I was. My mother disapproved, not only because he was a *cholo*, a gang member, but because he was older than I. He was 19, and I was only 14. But that didn't matter to me. All I cared about was having the love that I had missed for so long.

13   That was the best time. I had my friends in the gang, I had a boyfriend, and everything seemed fun and exciting. But then the partying ended, and I began to experience the real *vida loca*, the crazy life that is the reality of being in a gang. I had heard about drive-by shootings and killings, but such things seemed far away from me. When I was asked to help by hiding weapons for our *vatos*, our boys, I felt I had no choice. The *familia* took care of me, so I needed to take care of them, too. I began to see friends of mine die violent deaths at the hands of our "enemies." Now I realize they were not our enemies at all. They were low-income kids like us, scared and struggling to survive.

14   This was what my life in the gang was like for about a year. Then, when I was 15, I found I was pregnant. I went nearly crazy with panic. What was I supposed to do next? How would I tell my mother? Should I wait until my pregnancy was obvious or tell her now? Would she kick me out? How would I support this child? Would Sam leave me,

or would he stay? Should I have this baby or have an abortion? No! I knew at least the answer to that last question. I needed to face up to my responsibilities.

15   Being pregnant at such an early age created many difficult and shameful experiences for me. But it served another purpose. It was a wake-up call that made me look at my life and realize what bad shape I was in. I didn't want my child to see me this way, so I vowed to change. There would be no more parties, no more drugs, no more gang involvement.

16   On January 2, 1990, my son Cristian was born. I couldn't believe I was the mother of this beautiful baby. I was still a child myself, only 16 years old. And like a child, I blindly believed that life would hold only good things from now on. I had a man who loved me and a son who would make us a happy family. I was wrong.

17   Six months after Cristian was born,

Samuel and I were married. To marry then was not my choice, but my family was sick of hearing bad things about my being an unwed mother. Soon my relationship with Samuel began to deteriorate°. When Sam lost his job and the bills started to mount up, things got even worse. Sam became abusive to the point that I had black eyes and bruises. I have vivid memories of my husband beating me, slapping me, calling me foul names, telling me I was worth nothing. "Stop, stop, please stop!" I screamed with all my strength. Sometimes as I lay there taking his kicks and slaps, I wished he would kill me. I thought my life was over. I was only 17.

18   Abuse does strange things to a person. I thought it was all my fault. People told me, "Maybe you should cook better meals," "Maybe you should keep the house cleaner," or "Maybe you should stop saying things that make him angry." And I believed it. I thought if I did or said the right things, I could make him change. I felt as if the real me was disappearing because I was trying so hard to turn myself into somebody else, somebody who wouldn't make Samuel angry all the time.

19   Somehow, in the midst of my depression, I did manage to do one good thing for myself—I applied to a school for teenage mothers. After six months of being on a waiting list, I was notified of my acceptance.

20   Beginning school represented a turning point for me. I seized this opportunity to improve my life and change the way I looked at myself. In June 1992, when I was finally able to walk up on the stage and receive my high-school diploma, I cried from happiness. I realized I was capable of achieving anything I set my mind to.

21   The most helpful part of the school program had been the parenting class.

The woman who taught it, Ruth, was a psychologist, and she helped me a lot. Other people I tried to talk to seemed to judge me. They'd say things like, "Well, you must like getting hit, or you'd leave him." Ruth wasn't like that. She just heard me out, rather than jumping in to tell me how to fix my life.

22   Eventually, I arrived at my own decision. I was a worthwhile person, and I would not tolerate° any more abuse. I was pregnant with our second child, and I was determined our baby would not witness the violence that our son had seen. I would not ask for respect; I would demand it.

23   From that day on, things changed. I don't mean my life turned into some kind of fairy tale. Samuel and I separated and lived apart for some time. When Samuel wanted to get back together, Ruth suggested that he first get some counseling on his own, which he did. Later, she urged us to get counseling together, and we did that, too. About a year later, we got back together and moved to San Diego, in part to get away from the pressure in L.A. to return to our old lives.

24   In counseling, I came to understand better why Samuel abused me. I say "understand," not "accept." I will never, ever, again accept being abused. Samuel and I both know it was up to him to find other ways to deal with his problems. But I realized that violence was the only way he had ever seen men deal with conflict. He saw his father beat his mother and other neighborhood men beat their wives. As a little boy, he'd hear from his mother, "Men don't cry! Don't ever let anyone see you cry!" He'd kept everything inside. When we were in conflict, all he wanted was to make me shut up. Hitting me made me shut up.

25   Things are so much better now. I've never seen Samuel like this before. In counseling we said things we'd never said—me because I was always afraid of angering him, him because he thought I would think him less of a man.

Yvonne and her husband, Samuel, shop for food with their children.

26   Everyone sees the change in Samuel and in us. But not everyone likes the changes, and that makes things very hard. For example, last Sunday we were at my uncle's. All the men were sitting down, and all the women were waiting on them. But I was busy with the baby, so I said to Sam, "Why don't you get yourself some food?" Samuel got his own food and got me a plate, too, and the other men started in on him. They said, "Oh, Samuel, you have become a sissy. Next thing, she'll have you mopping floors." Sam just laughed it off, saying, "Oh, she does that already." Later he told me, "I don't care what any of them say. If this is what it takes to save our family, I'm

going to do it." But I wish that we had the support of our families.

27 The changes we've made have affected our parenting, too. Before I took the parenting class, I believed what everyone around me said: "If you don't hit your children, they'll turn out bad." But in class I began learning new ways to deal with the children. After Samuel went to counseling, he began to understand those new ways, too. Now we are trying our best to parent our children in a better way, but we've still got to deal with our parents and relatives telling us, "You're spoiling them. If you don't hit them, they'll be bad kids."

28 But we know what we are doing is right. It gives me hope when I hear our five-year-old asking Samuel why he used to hit me, and hear Sam tell him, "That was wrong. I am sorry. It will not happen again."

29 Now, at the age of 22, I am the mother of two children and a recent graduate of Southwestern College. While a student there, I was chosen to participate in the Puente Project. Puente is a writing and counseling project designed to increase the number of Latino students transferring to universities. The Puente Project has helped me immeasurably. I've had the opportunity to attend conferences and discover leadership abilities I never knew I had. My new self-confidence made it possible for me to be elected senator for the Associated Students' Organization.

Also, I started the Latina Club at Southwestern. In the club we worked to raise awareness of issues that affect Latinas and offer assistance to women in need.

30 At present, a new challenge arises. I have started classes at the University of Southern California in Los Angeles, where I will continue to strive for my dreams. I will study sociology and, eventually, practice family law. I want to be able to give back to my community by helping women overcome painful life events that threaten to destroy their faith in themselves.

31 I am often tired beyond belief. I race from changing diapers and preparing meals to memorizing numbers and long, fancy words that I barely understand. People often ask me, "Why do you even bother with school?" There are really two answers to that question. One is that I want to break out of the mold that traditionally confines Mexican women. In this way, I can become a role model for other Latinas and low-income women. Secondly, I am motivated by my children. I want to provide a better life for them than was provided for me.

32 My children inspire me to keep aiming high. Without them, I doubt that I would have started the search for a better me. When I am depressed and exhausted, doubting my ability to go on, their faces appear in my mind. They give me the strength to rise from where I have fallen and to continue my journey.

Vocabulary Check

1. In which sentence would the word **haven** make sense?
   a. When I tried basketball, I found that I had a real _____ for the sport.
   b. The no-hunting area is a _____ for deer.
   c. The apartment would be warmer if you would patch the _____ in the window.

2. In which sentence would the word **devastated** make sense?
   a. The driver was _____, so he stopped at a gas station to ask directions.
   b. When the student saw the A on his paper, he felt _____.
   c. When the teacher snapped at her, the girl showed no emotion, but inside she felt _____.

3. In the sentence below, the word **seized** means
   a. took hold of.
   b. rejected.
   c. ignored.

   "I seized this opportunity to improve my life and change the way I looked at myself." (Paragraph 20)

Yvonne walks through a campus square on her way to a class at the University of Southern California.

4. In the sentence below, the word **strive** means
   a. suffer.
   b. struggle.
   c. leave.

   "I have started classes at the University of Southern California in Los Angeles, where I will continue to strive for my dreams." (Paragraph 30)

5. In the sentence below, the word **confines** means
   a. costs.
   b. helps.
   c. limits.

   "I want to break out of the mold that traditionally confines Mexican women." (Paragraph 31)

SCORE: **(Number correct)** _____ **x 20 =** _____ **%**

Reading Check

Central Point and Main Ideas

1. What is the central point of the reading?
   a. Counseling is a way for people to learn about their problems and how to deal with them.
   b. Yvonne and Samuel have learned that hitting is not a good way to discipline children.
   c. With the help of counseling, Yvonne put an end to physical abuse in her life and started working to better herself and others.

2. What is the main idea of paragraph 7?
   a. Yvonne and her mother visited a friend who attended their church.
   b. When Yvonne was molested, her mother did nothing about it.
   c. After being molested, Yvonne was at first too frightened to say anything about it.

3. What is the main idea of paragraph 13?
   a. Yvonne found friends and excitement in the gang.
   b. Yvonne was asked to help hide weapons used by the gang.
   c. Although gang life was fun at first, it became scary and dangerous.

4. What is the main idea of paragraph 26?
   a. In Yvonne's family, the women wait on the men.
   b. Yvonne and Samuel's struggle for a healthy family life is not supported by their families.
   c. Yvonne and Samuel's relatives have learned that Samuel helps Yvonne around the house.

Supporting Details

5. Yvonne became involved with her gang
   a. when she was in junior high school.
   b. after she married Samuel.
   c. when her son Cristian was born.

6. The "one good thing" Yvonne did for herself while she was depressed and being abused was
   a. facing the man who had molested her.
   b. applying to a school for teenage mothers.
   c. moving to San Diego.

7. When Yvonne suggested that Samuel get himself a plateful of food at her uncle's house, Samuel
   a. accused her of treating him like a sissy.
   b. struck her.
   c. got his own food and brought her some as well.

Conclusions

Conclusions

8. You can conclude from paragraph 11 that
   a. Yvonne had not felt respected until she joined the gang.
   b. Yvonne liked to fight with other women.
   c. Yvonne always felt like an outsider, even within the gang.

9. You can conclude from paragraph 24 that
   a. Yvonne was surprised that Samuel beat her.
   b. men in Samuel's family were encouraged to talk about their feelings.
   c. children copy the behavior of the grownups around them.

10. You can conclude from paragraph 27 that before Yvonne and Samuel went to counseling,
    a. they disciplined their children by hitting them.
    b. they refused to ever hit their children.
    c. they did not love their children.

SCORE: (Number correct) _____ x 10 = _____%

Questions for Thinking and Discussion

1. How would you describe Yvonne's mother? Was she a good parent, a bad parent, or a bit of both?

Yvonne checks a reference book in the university library.

*Posing with Yvonne are her mother, Josefina; her son, Cristian;
her daughter, Crystal; and her husband, Samuel.*

2. Yvonne says that in "a neighborhood where gangs are all there is[,] crackheads and gangsters are the only people you have to look up to." How do you think a child is affected by growing up in such a neighborhood? Where could such a child look for more positive role models?

3. In the early years of her marriage, Yvonne believed that Samuel's abusive behavior was her fault. Do you think abuse is ever the fault of the person who is being abused? Why, or why not?

Ideas for Writing

1. Yvonne and Samuel learned they don't have to hit to teach their children. What ways can you think of other than hitting to get children to behave? Imagine that you are an advice columnist and someone has written you this letter:

   When my husband and I were children, we were often smacked by our parents. We want our children to be good, but we don't want to use violence. What other methods can we use to get them to behave?

   Write a helpful answer to the parent. Explain two or three nonviolent ways for teaching children how to behave. Include examples to show what you mean.

2. Through counseling, Samuel came to understand that he had learned to use violence from the men in his life. What behavior have you learned—from parents, family, friends, or neighbors—that you would like to change? Write a paper titled "A Change I'd Like to Make in Myself." Explain what the behavior is and how changing it would improve your life.

3 / David McBeth

David McBeth always had trouble in school. His problems with speaking grew into problems with reading and writing. Attempts to help him catch up in school led to more embarrassment and discouragement. After David spent years feeling stupid, a surprising discovery turned his life around.

Words to Watch

temporary (3): lasting for a limited time
There are many *temporary* jobs at the mall during the December holidays.

mimic (6): imitate
Mockingbirds *mimic* the songs of other birds.

humiliation (12): loss of pride or self-respect
I felt *humiliation* when my best friend rejected me.

relieved (21): freed from worry or fear
The mail carrier was *relieved* to see that the barking dog was on a leash.

learning disability (24): a language problem that makes learning difficult
Some students have a *learning disability* that makes it hard for them to spell correctly.

David McBeth stands in front of the hospital for troubled youths where he was confined as a boy.

When I was a kid in Nevada, Missouri, I suffered from a speech disorder. For example, I said *sketti* for *spaghetti* and *nipkins* for *napkins*. I had no hope of pronouncing the word *specific*, which always came out *pacific*. Although the speech problem may sound like a small one, it led to a series of obstacles that almost kept me from achieving a happy life.

I remember that in the second grade I wanted to save myself from the embarrassment of being unable to pronounce *R*'s. So I would leave certain syllables out of words or not use those words at all. My teachers noticed my problem and placed me in our school's speech therapy program. Speech classes were held in a bright red van parked on the edge of our school's playground. Students called it the "retard van." None of my classmates were aware that I was in speech. I knew that if they found out, they'd tease and harass me. Since my sessions were right after recess, the only way to keep my secret was to hide when the recess bell rang. Every day, while the rest of the boys and girls were lining up, I would hide behind the van and hope that no one noticed me missing.

By third grade, my poor reading and writing skills had put me behind in class. This setback was seen by the school to be a temporary° result of my speech problems from the year before. My teachers felt that I was bright and would catch up in no time. However, as the year progressed, I experienced little improvement. My mother's response was to place me in a class for students with special learning problems. People from the regional mental health center came to the school and tested me. The results were mixed. On one hand, I had a high IQ; on the other, I had a problem reading words and poor hand-eye coordination. I was then moved from the red speech van to the well-known "retard class." I can still remember sitting in my new classroom, my former classmates pressing their faces up against the window, pointing at me and laughing.

4   To this day, I don't believe my mother could have possibly understood what being "sentenced" to this class was like. She must have meant well, but the other kids in the class had much greater problems than mine. Many of them drooled all over themselves. My "work" included going to the cafeteria by myself and catching beanbags tossed to me by the teacher. At the same moment she tossed, I had to toss one to her. Sometimes, my assignment would be to walk back and forth on a balance beam. It took weeks of promising to read more books before my mother allowed me back into my regular class.

5   Through fourth grade, the city of Nevada was the only town I had known. Then my mother, sister, and I moved over a hundred miles away to a city twice as large. My parents had been divorced since I was four, and my mother explained that the move was to get us away from our father's influence.

6   I started fifth grade in an unfamiliar school, feeling more alone than ever. Spelling lessons there included standing in front of the class and spelling a word. Under such pressure, it seemed I could never spell any words correctly. The word that gave me the most trouble was

Sedalia, the name of our new town. Other students had no such problems. They laughed at me every time I made a mistake. In addition, they would mimic° the way I talked. This made the spelling sessions even more stressful, and my speech got even worse. At recess or lunchtime, my classmates would call, "Hey, Stupid! Spell *dumb!*" or some other mean or simple word. I avoided them by sitting on the slanted cellar doors against a far wall.

Before long, I began faking illness on   7
spelling and reading days. This act worked for over a month. Then one day I said to my mother, "I've got diarrhea. If I go to school, I won't make it to the bathroom."

She grabbed me by the arm. "You're   8
going to school."

She drove me there herself and   9
dragged me to the principal's office. While I sat outside, Mother, my teacher,

and the principal talked. Then my teacher came out of the office.

10   "Follow me," she ordered.

11   I walked with her back into the classroom, making my way past everyone's stares to my seat at the back. The teacher took her place at the front, looking angry. "David," she asked, "why did you make it sound as if I wouldn't let you go to the bathroom? I understand you have diarrhea and may need to leave during class."

12   The whole class turned toward me, laughing. I felt horror, humiliation°, and shame, and my stomach turned over violently. I ran out into the hallway and threw up everywhere. When I think about that day now, I still feel the violent movement in my stomach and the shaking of my arms.

13   The next day I was terrified of returning to school. My mother had to drag me outside and force me into the car. But I was determined never to go back to the classroom. While she walked around the car, I locked both doors and held down the lock button on whichever door she tried to open. She finally went next door for help. She gave the man a set of keys so they could unlock the car from both sides. But I put my foot on one button and stretched across the seat, holding the other button with my finger. As they tried unsuccessfully to open the door, I just stared down into the seat of the car. They finally gave up, and the man gave her a ride to work.

14   I knew this wouldn't be the end of my mother's attempts to get me back to school. On mornings after that, I got up before her and blocked my bedroom door. The doorknob was too high for me to jam a chair beneath it. So using a pair of shoes and Mother's ankle weights, I made a platform to raise the chair up to the doorknob. I'd then leave the chair there until my mother left for work.

15   Mom finally said, "You have two choices. It's either school or a psychologist."

16   Since anything was better than school, I went to the psychologist. During my first session, he had to step outside for a minute. While he was gone, I barricaded the door with a towel rack and some electric wire I found in the office. When he came back, he couldn't get in. As he and the others tried to talk me out, I ignored them and looked through the window. I wanted desperately to be back in Nevada, where I had felt a certain amount of safety. I knew I couldn't get there by myself, so I removed the barricade.

17   My mother decided to send me to a hospital for troubled youths back in Nevada. The hospital, a three-story brick building, had screens over all the windows to stop people from getting out. Although my dad was still in Nevada and could visit me anytime, I never wanted visitors. I felt that if no one saw me, then no one would believe I was really there. I hated knowing I was in that place, let alone thinking about anyone else knowing it.

18   I soon adjusted to the environment of locked doors, barred windows, and the "quiet room." This room was where patients were sent for such acts as going to bed with clothes on, stealing, or trying to leave. Throughout the hospital, lines on the floor marked the areas where residents were allowed to be. Also, patients had to follow a system of privileges based on their behavior. At first, I didn't understand this system, but then I got a copy of the rules. For weeks, I played the game and became a model resident with the highest privileges. Eventually, the hospital could no longer find any reason to hold me.

19   Now that I was "cured," my mother wanted me back in Sedalia. However, I

stated that I was not going back to that school. The solution was a small Catholic school in Sedalia. Things went well there until I had to write a five-page paper that was to be shared with the class. I knew it was poorly written and filled with spelling and grammar errors. Since I couldn't bear to let anyone know how stupid I thought I was, I went back to my old habit of skipping school.

David shares a moment with his wife, Amy.

20   I was forced to meet with yet another therapist. After a session in which I drew pictures of trees, my "shrink" somehow decided that I needed to live with my father. I returned to Nevada and finished the school year with no major problems. But because my mother still had not given up custody, she was able to make me move back to Sedalia by the year's end. The only hopeful thing was that I was 12—almost the age when the courts would listen if I told them where I wanted to live.

21   Several years later, when I was ready for high school, I moved back to Nevada to live with my dad. I was relieved° to be back with my old friends. I did well except in classes that involved spelling, reading, and writing. To get by in those classes, I cheated on tests or didn't go to class or didn't turn in all my writing assignments. Just as bad, I would write so sloppily that no one would be able to judge whether or not the words were spelled right. Despite all this, I was pushed along from one class to the next and graduated from high school.

22   My family then expected me to go to college, so I did. In college I made many friends, many of whom turned out to be drinking buddies. After two dismal semesters, my academic advisor told me to take at least one semester off. I wound up taking three years off.

23   Out of school, I worked in nursing homes and met the girl I soon married. After we had a baby boy, I strained my back at work and was unable to lift even my six-month-old son. Out of work, I tried to find another job that didn't require lifting, but I had no luck. Suddenly, education became important to me.

24   I enrolled in Missouri Southern College, which was far from both Sedalia and Nevada. One of the first courses I took was in psychology. In class, we were assigned a chapter on learning problems. I found out in that chapter about a learning disability° that made it difficult for a person to speak, spell, read, and write correctly. The very next day, my history professor suggested that if any students had trouble keeping up with the reading, they should seek help at the Learning Center. I did. I was tested for a learning disability and told that I had one that affected my language skills. This discovery changed my life.

25   I finally had a reason to explain why school was so difficult for me. After years of being treated as if I were insane or dumb, I at last knew what was wrong with me. It's not that I was stupid; it's that I had a learning disability. Before, all I could do was blame myself, something I had done for years. Now I learned not to. It is scary to think that if I had not gone back to school, I would never have learned what caused me so much pain.

26   Today I see an English tutor at least once a week. To aid my spelling, I am allowed to use an electronic dictionary during essay tests. My wife, my son, and a new baby girl all support me as I face the learning struggle of each new day.

27   I am studying to be a teacher. I want to help high-school students avoid the frustrating mistakes I made. I have learned to look ahead. The kid who said *sketti* for *spaghetti* and *nipkins* for *napkins* sees nothing that cannot be overcome. I no longer need propped chairs or wire barricades to shelter and protect me from the rest of the world. I am out of those enclosures, and nothing can hold me back now.

Vocabulary Check

1. In which sentence would the word **temporary** make sense?
   a. Our parents are proud of their _____ marriage of thirty years.
   b. After the tooth is pulled, there may be some _____ swelling.
   c. Our dog is very sweet, but her _____ size scares the neighbors.

2. In which sentence would the word **mimic** make sense?
   a. On summer evenings, we like to _____ our dinner out on the front porch.
   b. Every night, the actor would _____ the audience by entering the stage walking on his hands.
   c. When his older sister giggled on the phone, the boy liked to _____ her by giggling into his hand.

3. In the sentences below, the word **harass** means
   a. congratulate.
   b. bother.
   c. help.

   "None of my classmates were aware that I was in speech. I knew that if they found out, they'd tease and harass me." (Paragraph 2)

David looks up from his work at a computer in the college's Learning Center.

4. In the sentence below, the word **barricaded** means
   a. decorated.
   b. removed from sight.
   c. blocked with something.

   "While he was gone, I barricaded the door with a towel rack and some electric wire I found in the office." (Paragraph 16)

5. In the sentence below, the word **model** means
   a. well-dressed.
   b. serving as a very good example.
   c. behaving very badly.

   "For weeks, I played the game and became a model resident with the highest privileges." (Paragraph 18)

SCORE: **(Number correct)** _____ x 20 = _____%

Reading Check

Central Point and Main Ideas

1. What is the central point of the reading?
   a. Special classes, speech therapy, and a period in a hospital did not do much to help David with his problems.
   b. It was very difficult for David to be put into special classes with extremely retarded children.
   c. After years of suffering, David finally understood why he had learning problems, and he was able to move on in life.

2. What is the main idea of paragraph 2?
   a. David did everything he could to hide his reading problems from the other children.
   b. Speech classes were conducted in a red van parked at the edge of the playground.
   c. David tried to hide behind the red van at the end of recess so other students wouldn't know about his speech classes.

3. What is the main idea of paragraph 6?
   a. David attended fifth grade in a new school.
   b. Fifth grade was a horrible experience for David.
   c. Spelling lessons were difficult for David.

Supporting Details

4. When David's mother tried to force David to go to school, he
   a. hid inside the red van.
   b. locked himself in his mother's car.
   c. ran away to his father's house.

5. When David was enrolled in a small Catholic school, he would skip school because he
   a. was ashamed of his spelling and writing.
   b. was upset over his parents' divorce.
   c. hated going to math class.

6. David decided to try college a second time when he
   a. injured his back and could not return to his old job.
   b. took a test that showed he could do well in college.
   c. met a friend from high school who offered to enroll with him.

Conclusions

7. You can conclude from paragraph 3 that
   a. David's schoolmates teased him less after he was placed in the special class.
   b. David's teachers at first did not understand that he had serious learning problems.
   c. David knew that the class for students with special learning problems was the best place for him.

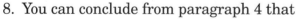

Playing with David are his son, Thomas, and his daughter, Lauren.

8. You can conclude from paragraph 4 that
   a. the work David was assigned was childish and useless.
   b. David was glad to be doing such easy work.
   c. the work may have been easy, but it was very helpful to David.

9. You can conclude from paragraph 23 that
   a. David regrets getting married when he did.
   b. David felt education could lead to a job that did not require heavy physical work.
   c. David's back was permanently injured.

10. You can conclude from paragraph 26 that
    a. David no longer has a learning disability.
    b. now that David understands his learning disability, he has no problems with his classes.
    c. understanding his problems makes it easier for David to deal with them.

SCORE: (Number correct) _____ x 10 = _____ %

David meets with his English tutor, Trisa Moss.

Questions for Thinking and Discussion

1. When David's classmates discovered he was in a special class, they made fun of him. Why do you think people, in general, tease others who are different in some way? What do you think would make them stop teasing?

2. Do you think David was right to refuse to go to school? Why or why not?

3. Why do you think it was such a relief to David when he learned that he had a learning disability? How did the discovery affect his life?

Ideas for Writing

1. All of us, at one time or another, have had to struggle with something that everyone else seems to do easily. Maybe we have trouble understanding a school subject, playing a sport, or meeting new people. Write a paper about one thing that is difficult for you. Describe how you feel when you have such trouble.

2. Whom have you known that was "different," like David? How was that person different? How did people around him or her act? How did you act? Write a paper answering these questions.

When Gwen Dasher was young, she was taken from her mentally ill mother and placed in one unhappy foster home after another. Despite many painful years, Gwen did not let the lack of loving adults in her world crush her hopes for the future. Now, as a wife, mother, and college student, she is breaking a pattern that could easily have gone on for generations.

4 / Gwendolyan Dasher

Words to Watch

cringed (4): shrank back (as in fear)
The frightened dog *cringed* when I reached out to pet her.

bizarre (7): strange
My brother's *bizarre* habits include eating popcorn for breakfast.

siblings (11): brothers and sisters
The *siblings* all have red hair like their father's.

excelled (11): were outstanding
Our old neighbors *excelled* at gardening. They grew beautiful flowers every year.

flexible (17): capable of change
Our team's practice hours are *flexible*. Practice can end as early as 4:30 or as late as 6:00 p.m.

Gwen Dasher visits with her mother.

I clearly remember the day when the police took me away from my mother. We six children were with her in our filthy, rat-infested apartment. She was wearing the only coat she owned. It was dark gray and trimmed in black fake fur. I thought it was beautiful. 1

A knock sounded at the front door. "Who is it?" my mother called. 2

"The police," answered a stern male voice. 3

I cringed°, looking at my mother. She opened the door, my baby sister in her arms, as I peeked out from behind her. A tall police officer stood in the door. To my child's eyes, he looked mean. With him were two women. 4

"Mrs. Moore," the officer said, "we are here with a court order to take your children into state's custody for neglect." 5

My mother let out such a scream that today, at age 34, I can still hear it. As she screamed, the officer grabbed my sister out of her arms and passed her to the woman waiting beside him. He barged into the apartment, collected all of us children, and hurried us out the door. 6

That day was one of anguish and terror. But I also felt relieved that adults were finally taking charge of a situation that threatened to overwhelm me. I was only a little girl, somewhere between eight and ten years old. (That time in my life 7 was so full of confusion that I honestly am not sure when it took place.) But being the oldest of six children meant that an enormous amount of responsibility had been laid upon me already. Over many months, I had watched in horror and confusion as my mother changed from a normal mom into a stranger with a bizarre° personality. Eventually her mind was so damaged that when she received her welfare check (our large family's only means of survival), she would cash the check and stick the money in her brassiere. There it would stay as the bills went unpaid and the refrigerator remained empty. Sometimes I would try to take the money from her bra as she slept so I could go buy food. Many times the man from the electric company came to turn off our lights. Many times I felt the embarrassment of having to pick up free food boxes or donated back-to-school clothes.

8   In elementary school, I didn't do very well academically. Now I know why—I was always hungry. For example, I remember one day when I went to the kitchen for food, but the refrigerator was empty. I searched the cupboards, but all I found was a blue box of Morton's salt. Sitting at the kitchen table, I poured mounds of the white salt into my hand and licked it until I couldn't bear the salty taste anymore.

9   When a classmate would invite me home to have dinner and play, I accepted eagerly. There I would get a decent meal and, perhaps, save something to take home to the others.

10   "Aren't I somebody? Why is this happening to me?" These were the questions I asked myself. As a child, there were few answers to my questions. For a long time, I blamed my mother for everything. I wondered why she didn't just get her mind fixed so my family could be together and happy. As I grew older, I learned that

she had suffered a nervous breakdown, but had never received any medical or psychological help. Her mental problems had developed into serious mental illness. By that time, she was as unable to help herself as I was.

The crazy life with my mother ended 11 the day the police collected my siblings° and me. We were placed in foster care. I'd like to say that my life then became happy, normal, and stable, but that was not the case. In my first foster home, I was just a monthly check. No one cared where I was or what I did, as long as that check arrived. Later I was placed in a different home along with one of my younger sisters. At first, I was happy because at least I was with a sibling. But that home was hell on earth. My life was like that of Cinderella, only this was no fairy tale with a happy ending. I was that family's gold mine and live-in slave. My foster parents excelled° in mental and verbal abuse. They taunted me about my weight. The money intended to support me was spent instead on my foster mother's adopted daughter. She had private school, expensive clothes, fourteen-carat gold jewelry, and piano lessons. I had no life as a child at all. High school was very difficult. There I was mocked as overweight and poorly dressed in a school full of students from well-off families.

12 Now that I look back, I believe the cruel things my fellow students and foster parents did made me a stronger person. "Just you wait and see," I would silently answer them, "I am somebody." Reading about Jesse Jackson and his message to young people strengthened that belief in myself: "I am somebody." Reading the Bible and autobiographies of other African-American leaders provided me with a safe haven and a strong will to live. As I read the Bible, I wondered why my life had been so sad. How could a child have committed any sin so great as to deserve all this hardship? Reading the autobiographies, I imagined I was one of the characters in the book, not a child in foster care. Such fantasies provided me with a few minutes of peace and calm.

13 As soon as I turned 18, I withdrew myself from the foster-care system. I enrolled in junior college but became so involved with my new freedom and with trying to find my siblings that I soon withdrew from school. A full-time job in the electronics industry was my next step. I married at age 22 and began a family. Eventually, I realized that to advance at work, I needed more education. I started junior college classes again, this time part-time at night.

14 My life today is pretty normal. My husband and I have the usual struggles as we try to balance work, marriage, parenting, and my schooling, but those are challenges I'm glad to deal with. My husband,

a fiber-optics technician, and I have two wonderful children. I don't talk to them much about my own childhood. I want to share the happy parts of my life with them rather than the sad ones. Because of what I experienced, I am probably more concerned than many parents with providing my son and daughter with lots of affection and self-esteem. Not having been raised with those things myself, I take the time to read books and articles and even attend classes on good parenting.

15 My mother lives in a group home for people with mental illness. I administer her finances, so the children and I visit her fairly often, but she is not able to have much of a caring relationship with anyone. I'm used to that, but I still struggle with it at times, especially when I see a woman my age enjoying the company of her own mother. I suppose I'll always wish I could have that maternal support, to be able to call my mom and say, "Listen to what the children did now." That's a loss that I feel even today.

16 Although my siblings and I haven't had the close ties we would if we had grown up together, I think that is slowly changing. Now, as adults, we're building our relationships. I'm the "rounder-upper"—I get everyone together for family get-togethers. For instance, we all took our mother to a restaurant for Mother's Day recently.

17 I'm now a student at Ottowa University in Phoenix, Arizona. I've done well in school, better than I ever imagined possible. This semester I earned a B average, and I am determined to continue until I have earned a bachelor's degree in Human Resource Management. I'm pretty flexible° about my career goals, but right now I'm hoping to work in the health field or in public relations. I feel confident that once I get my degree, I can handle just about anything.

18   That's the good news. The bad news is that my employment recently ended. The unsteady nature of the electronic and aerospace industries led my employer to lay off many workers. I'm working part-time as a phone operator in a hospital, and once again I am finding it difficult to attend college, this time because money is tight in my household.

19   But I will find a way. A college education will make me a more positive role model for my children. It will make me better qualified for satisfying, lasting employment. Maybe most important of all, it will allow me to look back upon the horrible environment I came out of and say, "My past did not defeat me. I rose above it. I am somebody. And still I rise."

Posing with Gwen are her husband, William, Jr.; her son, William, III; and her daughter, Courtney.

Vocabulary Check

1. In which sentence would the word **bizarre** make sense?
   a. A school _____ was held to raise money for new gym equipment.
   b. In our dreams, _____ behavior often seems very normal.
   c. Yesterday the weather was so _____ that we decided to go on a picnic.

2. In which sentence would the word **excelled** make sense?
   a. Although my brother _____ in sports, I am not very athletic.
   b. My friend _____ at math, so his teacher suggested that he get some tutoring.
   c. After the movie, the audience _____ through the back doors.

3. In the sentence below, the word **barged** means
   a. tiptoed.
   b. were welcomed.
   c. rudely entered.

   "[The officer] barged into the apartment, collected all of us children, and hurried us out the door." (Paragraph 6)

4. In the sentence below, the word **taunted** means
   a. made fun of.
   b. complimented.
   c. asked.

   "[My foster parents] taunted me about my weight." (Paragraph 11)

5. In the sentences below, the word **administer** means
   a. question.
   b. delay.
   c. manage.

   Gwen studies at home for one of her college classes.

   "My mother lives in a group home for people with mental illness. I administer her finances, so the children and I visit her fairly often. . . . " (Paragraph 15)

SCORE: (Number correct) _____ x 20 = _____%

Reading Check

Central Point and Main Ideas

1. What is the central point of the reading?
   a. Despite a lack of adult support in the past, Gwen has built a normal life as a caring wife, parent, daughter, and sister.
   b. Mental problems can develop into serious mental illnesses.
   c. Having had a mentally ill mother and cruel foster parents, Gwen experienced a very difficult childhood.

2. What is the main idea of paragraph 7?
   a. Gwen's mother often did not pay her electric bill.
   b. Gwen had to wear donated clothes to school and sometimes had to pick up free food boxes for her family.
   c. Despite her fear, Gwen was glad adults took charge of her family because her mother was not capable of doing so.

3. What is the main idea of paragraph 11?
   a. Gwen's foster parents were paid for taking care of her.
   b. Life as a foster child was not happy for Gwen.
   c. High-school students can be cruel and thoughtless.

Supporting Details

4. How old was Gwen when she was taken from her mother's custody?
   a. 5
   b. Between 8 and 10
   c. Between 14 and 16

5. How did Gwen comfort herself when her foster parents and fellow students made fun of her?
   a. She read the Bible and stories of African-American leaders.
   b. She became an outstanding athlete.
   c. She volunteered in a home for the mentally ill.

6. Gwen's mother now lives
   a. with Gwen.
   b. in a group home for mentally ill people.
   c. alone.

Conclusions

7. You can conclude from paragraph 10 that
   a. nervous breakdowns are very rare.
   b. Gwen thought she was to blame for her mother's mental illness.
   c. Gwen no longer blames her mother for her strange behavior.

8. You can conclude from paragraph 13 that
   a. as an older teenager, Gwen had learned to like being a foster child.
   b. Gwen did not want to work in the electronics industry.
   c. Gwen had lost touch with most of her siblings.

9. You can conclude from paragraph 14 that
   a. Gwen believes people who did not *have* good parents need to learn to *be* good parents.
   b. Gwen's husband does not believe she should attend college.
   c. Gwen's children have very poor self-esteem.

10. You can conclude from paragraph 16 that
    a. Gwen's siblings dislike each other very much.
    b. Gwen never goes to her siblings' houses.
    c. strong family ties are important to Gwen.

SCORE: (Number correct) _____ x 10 = _____%

Questions for Thinking and Discussion

1. Neither Gwen's mother nor her foster parents were what most people would consider good parents. In your opinion, what makes a good parent? Think of two or three qualities that you think are important in a parent. Be ready to explain why you think those qualities matter so much.

A student at Ottowa University, Gwen meets with Virginia Boyle,
her teacher in a business management course.

Gwen tries to spend some time each day reading with her son.

2. As Gwen's experience shows, not all foster parents are well suited to their job. For that reason, some people would like to see children whose parents cannot raise them placed in group homes. Do you think children should be in group homes with other children like themselves? Or should they be in private homes? What do you think would be the good points and bad points of each type of home?

3. Gwen was mocked by other students because she was overweight and poorly dressed. Why do you think people make fun of those who are different?

Ideas for Writing

1. During difficult times, Gwen raised her spirits by imagining herself as a character in stories about African-American leaders. Who do you daydream about being? Write a paper describing what person you would like to be, and why.

2. Write a letter to an adult in your life who has inspired or supported you. Thank that person for what he or she has done, and explain what the inspiration or support has meant to you. The adult might be someone you know personally, or he or she might be a well-known figure whom you admire.

Juan Angel's life in rural Mexico was filled not with toys and books, but with hard work and abuse. Forced to do a man's work as a boy, Juan learned to work with his mind as well as his hands. Struggling for every bit of his education, he has successfully overcome one difficulty after another.

5 / Juan Angel

Words to Watch

stocky (3): thickly built
It is hard to find clothes for my son because he is so *stocky*.

relented (14): gave in; yielded
My boss did not want to give me a raise but *relented* after he heard I had another job offer.

averse (17): strongly unwilling (to do something); reluctant
The parents were *averse* to taking their daughter to the scary movie.

frail (17): weak
The *frail* patient had to be lifted from the wheelchair.

formidable (21): difficult to overcome
Being five feet, two inches tall is a *formidable* disadvantage on the basketball court.

Juan Angel studies at home.

In a rare moment of rest in the living room of his crowded trailer home, Juan Angel smiles as he watches his children play. His days are busy with work, school, and the demands of raising a family. But he shrugs off the idea that he tries to cram too much into every twenty-four-hour day. "That's life," he says. And he continues to do what he has done since he was a small child in rural Mexico. In the face of every challenge, he just keeps going. ₁

Juan's struggle began when he was two years old. His father, an alcoholic, abandoned the family. Left without means to support her child, Juan's mother was forced to leave him with an uncle so she could go to the United States in search of work. By the age of 3, Juan found himself in an unfamiliar village without either of his parents and without any protection from the man who was supposed to be his guardian—his uncle. ₂

Juan's uncle was a mean man. To him, Juan was a source of labor. When he was 4, Juan was forced to cut wood, using a large, curved knife called a machete. At the age of 5, he worked in a distillery, helping to produce cheap wine. All the money that Juan earned went to his uncle. His uncle's "payment" to him was beatings and insults. "You're fat and lazy," his uncle would tell Juan as he struck him with his fists. "You'll never ₃ amount to anything." Even Juan's cousins, his uncle's children, mistreated him, making fun of how short and stocky° he was. When Juan told his uncle how the other kids teased him, his uncle would ignore him, or worse. Sometimes he would respond by making Juan sleep outside.

4   During one of those cold, lonely nights outside, after an especially bad beating, Juan decided he had to leave. He ran several miles to the safety of the house of his grandmother. He was 8 years old.

5   His grandmother acted as if she did not believe Juan's stories about his uncle. But she did allow him to stay in her home. Juan's grandmother was kinder than his uncle, but his life was still not easy. His grandmother raised pigs for a living, and because she was growing older, she needed someone to care for the animals. Juan's days were filled with hard labor. He rose at dawn to feed and water the pigs. During the day, he took a donkey and an axe and searched for firewood to sell. In the evening, he kept his grandmother's house neat and clean. At the age of 9, Juan was doing the work of an adult.

6   One morning while Juan was feeding the pigs, he noticed two boys from another village walking by. They carried canvas bags on their shoulders.

7   "What are you two doing?" Juan asked.

8   "We're going to school," they said.

9   The idea of going to school was foreign to Juan. Not one child from his grandmother's village of ten houses had ever gone to school.

10   Juan didn't believe the boys until they pulled some paper from their bags and drew strange lines on it. "Writing," they called it. They read aloud to him from their books. Juan stared in wonder.

They told him that he could learn to read and write too and that he should go with them.

11   That night Juan told his grandmother about the boys and asked if he, too, could go to school.

12   "Absolutely not!" she answered. "Forget about going to school. You must stay here and care for the pigs." Even when Juan came up with a plan to care for the pigs and attend school, she refused.

13   For two more years, Juan tended the pigs. Pouring their corn slop into the trough, he would watch the two boys walking to school and dream about all they were learning. Occasionally, they would stop and talk to Juan, still encouraging him to go to school. They told him about a friend who lived behind the school. "You could live there," they said. Juan looked at the options before him. He was torn by guilt whenever he considered leaving his grandmother alone. But he knew what staying meant—a lifetime of poverty, feeding pigs, and chopping wood.

14   Finally, without telling his grandmother, Juan left his village and went with the boys. He moved into their friend's house and went to his first day of classes. He was the oldest child in the school. Standing in line with the other kids, he noticed them staring and whispering about him. The principal soon pulled him aside and explained that Juan was too old for the school. But Juan would not give up. After he explained his story and how much he wanted an education, the principal relented°. If Juan could keep his grades up, he could attend school.

15   One week later, after days of searching, Juan's grandmother found him. She was silent and angry as she approached the school. Juan was sure that she would

force him to leave. However, after a long time in the office with the principal, his grandmother announced that Juan could stay. All she asked was that he continue to complete his chores and care for the pigs. He hugged her happily, grateful for her understanding.

16   Juan kept his end of the bargain. For the next six years, he got up every morning at 5:30, fed and watered the pigs, and walked the two miles to school. Sometimes he was teased by the village kids for going to school. On occasion, they even beat him. But Juan Angel kept going. Finally he graduated from primary school, the first in his family ever to do so.

17   Juan wanted to go on with his education, but the nearest high school was a three-hour bus trip away. He knew he would rarely be able to afford the trip

home, and he was averse° to leaving his grandmother so completely alone. However, she encouraged him to go. She even managed to buy him some new clothes out of her tiny savings. With mixed feelings, Juan said goodbye to his grandmother and left for his new school. On his rare trips back to the village, he noticed sadly how old and frail° she was becoming.

18   One night, during his third year of high school, a friend from home arrived and warned him that his grandmother was very weak. Juan borrowed money for bus fare and left for home. He found his grandmother—too poor to have a bed or sofa—lying on the floor, covered by a thin blanket.

19   When she saw Juan, her face lit up, and she hugged him. With tears in his eyes, he listened to her instructions not to cry but to stay in school, to study hard, to keep going. She died in his arms the next day.

20   Obeying his grandmother's wish, Juan Angel kept going and finished secondary school. While there, he met and married his wife, and they had a child. After a long, unsuccessful search for work, Juan was forced into the same decision his mother had made long ago. He said goodbye to his family, boarded a bus, left Mexico, and went to join his mother in Oregon.

21   In the United States, Juan found himself in a bewildering world. Usually simple tasks like going to the grocery store, asking for directions, or reading signs became formidable° barriers. For eight days Juan searched for a job, isolated by his inability to understand the language and culture around him. On the verge of returning to Mexico in defeat, Juan remembered the lessons of his past and relied on what he knew could help him: school.

22   Juan enrolled in an English class at a local high school, where he studied intensely three nights a week. He found a job on an alfalfa farm, spending as much as seventeen hours a day watering, stacking, and baling alfalfa. The work was very hard, but his dedication to school never wavered. He earned his high-school general equivalency diploma and saved enough money to bring his family to Oregon.

23   And he just kept going. Learning English and working on a farm were not enough for Juan. He wanted a better future for himself and his family. As a result, he quit his farm job and took one at a feed processing plant. His new schedule allowed him to take classes at Blue Mountain Community College.

24   Today Juan is still in college. Between his forty hours a week at the plant and his three college courses, Juan has difficulty finding time for his wife, his three children, and his homework. While his family supports his efforts, not everyone understands his need to learn. Sometimes his bosses reprimand him for reading a textbook on his lunch break. His coworkers shake their heads when he studies for an exam between loading trucks with livestock feed.

25   At night, sitting in his trailer home, Juan knows the struggle is not over. He still has a year of college. He wants a better job. He wants to spend more time with his family. "You just have to keep going," he says, and he will. He always does. Smiling as his son, two-year-old Danny, toddles by, Juan sinks back wearily into his chair. Tomorrow there will be more work, more classes, more homework, more family that needs him. And, somehow, he'll manage it all. After all, as Juan Angel reminds himself, "That's life."

On his job at the alfalfa farm, Juan spent part of his time repairing harvest equipment.

Vocabulary Check

1. In which sentence would the word **formidable** make sense?
   a. The young boxer had a _____ opponent—a man with twice as much experience.
   b. It was _____ of my parents to have all the neighborhood children over for a party.
   c. Fixing the squeaking door is a _____ job that will take me only seconds to do.

2. In which sentence would the word **frail** make sense?
   a. The _____ door was six inches thick.
   b. The _____ sound of the thunder woke me out of a deep sleep.
   c. A _____ branch sagged from the weight of several apples.

3. In the sentences below, the word **bewildering** means
   a. funny.
   b. confusing.
   c. criminal.

   "In the United States, Juan found himself in a bewildering world. . . . simple tasks like going to the grocery store, asking for directions, or reading signs became formidable barriers." (Paragraph 21)

With Juan and his wife, Hilda, are their children (left to right), Vianey, Danny, and Juan, Jr.

4. In the sentence below, the word **isolated** means
   a. separated from others.
   b. entertained.
   c. chased.

   "For eight days Juan searched for a job, isolated by his inability to understand the language and culture around him." (Paragraph 21)

5. In the sentences below, the word **reprimand** means
   a. compliment.
   b. ignore.
   c. scold.

   "Not everyone understands his need to learn. Sometimes his bosses reprimand him for reading a textbook on his lunch break." (Paragraph 24)

SCORE: **(Number correct)** _____ x 20 = _____%

Reading Check

Central Point and Main Ideas

1. What is the central point of the reading?
   a. Juan's grandmother changed her mind about letting him going to school.
   b. Juan has not let anything stop him from getting an education and supporting his family.
   c. Juan eventually became the first person in his family to graduate from primary school.

2. What is the main idea of paragraph 3?
   a. When Juan was very young, his life was filled with hard work and abuse.
   b. Juan's cousins followed their father's example by being cruel to Juan.
   c. Small children should not be forced to do adult work, such as cutting wood.

3. What is the main idea of paragraph 14?
   a. Despite discouragement, Juan finally managed to attend school.
   b. Juan did not tell his grandmother he was leaving her village to go to school.
   c. The principal told Juan that he was too old to be going to a primary school.

Supporting Details

4. Juan's grandmother wanted Juan to stay home from school and care for her
   a. donkeys.
   b. cattle.
   c. pigs.

5. Juan was surprised that the two boys passing his house were going to school because
   a. they seemed too old to be students.
   b. nobody from his grandmother's village had ever gone to school.
   c. he knew the boys often lied.

6. As Juan's grandmother lay dying, she asked him to
   a. quit school and return to live with her.
   b. stay in school.
   c. join his mother in the United States.

7. Juan quit his job on a farm and took one at a feed processing plant because
   a. his bosses at the farm criticized him for studying during his breaks.
   b. the pay at the feed plant was better than on the farm.
   c. the schedule of his new job allowed him to go to college.

Conclusions

8. You can conclude from paragraphs 3, 4, and 5 that
   a. Juan never really had a childhood.
   b. Juan enjoyed learning how to raise pigs.
   c. Juan's uncle often behaved cruelly to Juan's grandmother.

9. You can conclude from paragraph 15 that
   a. Juan's grandmother never forgave him for running away to school.
   b. the principal must have encouraged Juan's grandmother to let Juan stay in school.
   c. Juan's grandmother could have afforded to hire someone to do Juan's chores and care for her pigs.

10. You can conclude from paragraph 20 that
    a. Juan and his mother had kept in touch.
    b. there were plenty of jobs in Mexico.
    c. Juan did not really want to work in Mexico.

SCORE: **(Number correct)** _____ x 10 = _____%

Questions for Thinking and Discussion

1. Juan grew up in an area of Mexico where children did not have many of the advantages that most American children take for granted. Were you surprised by what Juan's childhood was like? What surprised you most about his experience?

2. How did you feel about Juan's grandmother when she refused to let him attend school? Why do you think she refused? Did your opinion of her change as the story went on?

3. Juan worked very hard to go to school, to live in the U.S., and to learn English. What do you think motivates him? Why is it so important to him, as the story says, "to keep going"?

At home, Juan lets his daughter, Vianey, share a few moments on his computer.

In the background is the feed processing plant
where Juan presently works.

Ideas for Writing

1. Juan's uncle was a cruel man. Have you ever witnessed an example of mean or cruel behavior? Maybe it was directed at you, or maybe it was directed against someone else. Write a paper describing what happened and how you reacted.

2. Imagine not being able to read or write. Write a paper describing how a day in your life would be affected by your inability to read or write.

6 / Claire Henson

Words to Watch

assure (10): promise
Can you *assure* me you'll be on time for work?

prohibited (11): prevented
Poor health *prohibited* my grandmother from coming to the wedding.

vulnerable (15): open to being tempted or persuaded
Because I was hungry, I felt *vulnerable* when I passed the fast-food restaurant.

upheaval (28): disturbance
It can take years to overcome the *upheaval* caused by a hurricane.

immersed (29): deeply involved
My brother was so *immersed* in his book that he didn't hear me call him for dinner.

Claire Henson studies one of her college textbooks.

On August 23, 1973, I came into this world fighting for my life. I was a premature baby, weighing only four pounds. I was choking on the blood that filled my inadequately formed lungs. The hospital staff hooked me up to life-support equipment and warned my father that I was unlikely to survive.

When my mother became more alert after her labor medications wore off, she was informed that her newborn daughter was struggling for survival. The hospital physicians gave me a 50 percent chance to live. If I did survive, I had a 50 percent chance of being mentally retarded. Disobeying her doctor's strict orders to stay in bed, my mother weakly walked to the nursery windows. She peered through the glass, hoping to catch a glimpse of the child she might never hold.

To everyone's surprise, I quickly become stronger and healthier. The doctors were amazed at my recovery, but they warned my parents I might still suffer from some learning disabilities.

The doctors were right. When I entered first grade, I was bewildered. Puzzles didn't make sense to me. Numbers and letters that other children seemed to understand were just jumbles. In order to stay afloat, I often copied work from my neighbors' papers. When my teacher handed back my work with big fat *X*'s all over it, I was proud. I thought those *X*'s meant my work was perfect!

5 As the school year progressed, my teacher recommended that I be placed in a pre-first classroom. This class was designed for children who were not ready for the challenge of first grade. The slower pace and greater teacher attention of pre-first were perfect for me. I began to catch up with the other students, and when it was time to try first grade again, I was ready.

6 Why was my birth so difficult? And why did I have so many problems learning when I was little? At the time, no one was saying. It was just "one of those things." But as I grew older, I began to form my own opinions. My father and mother were both alcoholics. I believe that alcoholism nearly cost me my life as a newborn and caused my learning disabilities. From the moment I was born, alcohol has negatively influenced my life.

7 Children become accustomed to what they live with. Normal for my family was a house where alcohol was always present. Normal was a mother who was always at the bar instead of at home. Normal was my sister and I trying to protect the Christmas presents we were wrapping as my parents fought in the living room.

8 But even for us, one incident stood out as strange. That was the night that Dad loaded me and my sisters into the car. We were wearing our pajamas. We all drove to the bar and went in, looking for my mom. Dad asked her to come home, but she wouldn't. We drove back home. Then Dad took all her belongings—even the hair-styling equipment she used for work—and threw them out on the lawn. After that, my mom took us girls and moved into an apartment, and she and my father got divorced.

9 My mother worked while my older sister Tammy, who was 13, watched my younger sister Kim, who was 7, and me. But soon it wasn't only during Mom's working hours that we were on our own. Her after-work visit to the bar stretched late into the evening. Then she started disappearing for days on end, sometimes even for a week. Our communication consisted of brief phone calls and notes left on the kitchen table. We might see her when she dropped off a few groceries. Other times there were no groceries; my sisters and I mixed eggs and flour to make pancakes more than once.

10 I kept trying to believe she would live up to her promises. Year after year, in the fall, she made a date to take us shopping for back-to-school clothes. "I'll take you tomorrow when you get home from school," she would promise. At 3:30, we would get off the bus, grab a snack, and sit eagerly waiting for her car to

arrive. Around 6:00, she might call, saying something like, "I'm just having a few beers with a friend—I'll be there in an hour." Hours later, when it was obviously too late to go, we'd call her at the bar. "We'll go another day," she would carelessly assure° us.

11 After I became a teenager, I began to take advantage of my lack of adult supervision. School became a meeting place for me and my friends, rather than a place to learn. During weekends, my mother was never home. She tried to enforce a midnight curfew by telephoning me at that time. However, I soon realized that as long as I was home to take her call, nothing prohibited° me from leaving again. I spent the night with friends, including my girlfriend Megan, often partying until the early morning hours.

12 My family's lives revolved around alcohol. When my sisters and I were children, we were like little barmaids. It was always, "Claire, pour me a glass of wine with plenty of ice." But, believe it or not, the subject of alcohol abuse was never mentioned in our family. Just once during those years did I try to confront my mother about her drinking. As soon as I mentioned the word "alcoholic," she exploded. "Do you know what an alcoholic is?" she screamed. "Yes," I said. "It's someone whose life and relationships are affected by her drinking." "No!" she insisted. "Who is putting these lies into your head? An alcoholic is someone who drinks from the moment they get up in the morning! I do not have a drinking problem!" That was the last time we ever talked about it.

13 By the time I was 16, there was nothing left of our mother-daughter relationship but hurt and tears. One weekend I broke my curfew, as usual. But this time I got caught. When the time came to talk about it, my mother was drunk and enraged. She threw me out of the house.

Not only that, she telephoned the police to inform them that she was no longer responsible for my welfare.

14 I moved in with my friend Megan and her family. After a week, my mother called me and wanted to come home. I too wanted to work things out, so I went home at the time we had agreed. She wasn't there. I waited through the night and all the next day. She didn't even call. At eleven o'clock the second night, I decided there was no point in waiting longer. I made arrangements to move in with Megan's family, this time on a permanent basis.

15 The year and a half I spent with Megan's family included some of the lowest and highest points of my life. Megan was a rebellious high-school dropout whose only goal was to have a good time. In my vulnerable° state, I was easily lured into her lifestyle. Soon I decided that I, too, would quit school and get a full-time job. At first I enjoyed being out of school, but after about five weeks of "freedom," I had a dream—a nightmare, actually—that turned my life around.

16 In my dream, I was living in a shelter for homeless teenagers. I was hungry, so I approached a man who was guarding a cupboard of food. The doors of the cabinet were open. Inside I could see three shelves. On the top shelf sat my favorite food, canned ravioli.

17 "Can I have some ravioli?" I asked.

18 "Have you graduated from high school?" he answered.

19 Shocked, I admitted I had not graduated, but told him that I planned to earn my general equivalency diploma. He shook his head. "If you didn't graduate from high school, you can't eat off the top shelf," he said. "You can have what's on the bottom."

20 I stared at the bottom shelf where he was pointing. It was empty except for one pea pod.

21   When I awoke, I felt as though an angel had visited me with a message. I knew from that moment that education was the key to my living a better life. Without it, I would be doomed to live the life of a lower-class citizen, taking whatever leftovers came my way. That same day I enrolled in the local high school.

22   Megan's parents were impressed by my commitment to turning my life around. Her stepfather helped me find a part-time job as a cashier in a lumber store, and he also helped me open a savings account. I then offered to pay rent to Megan's parents. Although they accepted it for a few weeks, they soon decided I should save my funds for my own needs. In return, I helped with household chores and often babysat Megan's three-year-old brother, Jesse.

23   As my self-confidence and self-respect grew, my relationship with Megan fell apart. I rarely went to parties with her any more since I was more interested in keeping up with my studies and my job. She resented my ability to buy my own clothes, and she reacted by "borrowing" my clothes and returning them ruined. Eventually Megan left town with a group of friends to follow the Grateful Dead concert tours.

24   During this time, I took my mother to court in an effort to obtain the child-support money that my father was still paying to her. The judge did not agree to that. He did, however, declare me an emancipated minor, which meant that my mother no longer had any legal control over me.

25   An important influence during my remaining years in high school was my counselor, Mr. DiNardo. He guided me into an alternative education program which allowed students to learn career skills. During my junior and senior years, I spent half my day learning about the nursing profession. I became secretary of the local chapter of a club called Health Occupational Students of America, and, later, was elected a state officer in the organization.

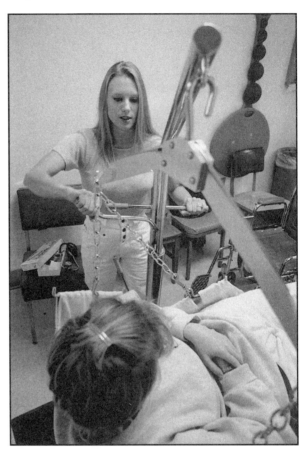

A physical therapy major, Claire learns how to operate a lifting device at school.

26   Mr. DiNardo also influenced my recovery as a child of an alcoholic. After hearing about my background, he suggested that I attend a meeting of his Children of Alcoholics (COA) support group. Even then, after all I had endured due to my mother's drinking, I denied there was alcoholism in my family, but he persisted. The first time I attended a COA meeting, I was surprised and relieved to find so many other teenagers who had had experiences similar to mine. At last, there were people with whom I could talk freely. As we laughed and cried together, I grew into a stronger person.

The pressures which continued in my life began to seem more manageable.

27   When I graduated from high school, I felt that I had earned not only a diploma but also a greater understanding of myself, my goals, and the disease of alcoholism. I saw leaving my mother's home as an act of survival, rather than rebellion. I believed I was on my way to a successful adult life.

28   My grades, however, had suffered during all the years of upheaval°. I desperately wanted to be accepted to a college nursing program, but my grades and my standardized test scores were dismally low. When I was turned down for acceptance at D'Youville College in Buffalo, New York, I was in despair. Where would I go now? What would I do? The answer came in a second letter from D'Youville. In it, I read about the Higher Education Opportunity Program (HEOP). This is a summer-long program to strengthen the skills of academically and financially disadvantaged students. I immediately applied for the program and was accepted. I graduated from high school on a Thursday. On the following Sunday, I was living in a dorm at D'Youville as a HEOP student.

29   The HEOP program helped me more than I can say. From 7:00 a.m. until 5:00 p.m. each day, I was immersed° in classes to improve my reading, writing, science knowledge, and computer skills. I learned about time management and study skills. By the time I entered D'Youville as a freshman in the fall, I was prepared to do well. I had felt that my high-school grades didn't reflect my abilities, and HEOP gave me the chance I needed to prove that to myself and others. I was now confident that if I tried hard, I would succeed. By the end of my freshman year, I was on the Dean's List. I had also been selected as a member of a college honor society.

30   Now I am starting my junior year as a student in D'Youville's Physical Therapy department. The junior year has the reputation of being the toughest in the program, so I know I will have to work hard. I am also active in Campus Ministry; other students and I get together to do things like clean shelters for the homeless, work in soup kitchens, and organize skating parties for the blind.

31   I feel I can never forget the alcoholism in my background. It is part of my life, now and forever. I have to to be careful about not unconsciously falling into harmful behavior patterns of children of alcoholics. The obvious mistake I could make is to become an abuser of alcohol myself. But in other, less obvious ways, I could harm myself, like having inappropriate relationships with other alcoholics or with someone I wanted to "parent" me.

32   I will not risk losing what I have accomplished by falling into those traps. My education is a privilege and a cherished gift. I will not waste it. By continuing to seek counseling and never forgetting the lessons I have learned, I am making sure that my life will be guided by positive choices. Alcoholism nearly cost me my life. I will not allow it to determine my future.

Vocabulary Check

1. In which sentence would the word **prohibited** make sense?
   a. Fear of heights has _____ me from ever going up in an airplane.
   b. After working as a bank teller for a year, I was _____ to a job as a loan officer.
   c. When the art teacher saw my drawings, she _____ me to sign up for advanced art classes.

2. In which sentence would the word **vulnerable** make sense?
   a. Advertisers know children are more _____ consumers when ads contain their favorite TV characters.
   b. My cousin is popular because he has such a _____ sense of humor.
   c. That girl is not only a good student, but she's also a _____ athlete.

3. In the sentence below, the word **inadequately** means
   a. perfectly.
   b. not sufficiently.
   c. permanently.

   "I was choking on the blood that filled my inadequately formed lungs." (Paragraph 1)

4. In the sentence below, the word **confront** means
   a. face.
   b. avoid.
   c. comfort.

Claire reads a book on campus.

   "Just once during those years did I try to confront my mother about her drinking." (Paragraph 12)

5. In the sentences below, the word **lured** means
   a. surprised.
   b. discouraged.
   c. attracted.

   "In my vulnerable state, I was easily lured into her lifestyle. Soon I decided that I, too, would quit school and get a full-time job." (Paragraph 15)

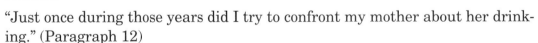

SCORE: (Number correct) _____ x 20 = _____%

Reading Check

Central Point and Main Ideas

1. What is the central point of the reading?
    a. Children of alcoholics often have many problems.
    b. With help and hard work, Claire overcame problems that were the result of her being the child of alcoholics.
    c. Schools should have more special programs such as Children of Alcoholics and the Higher Education Opportunity Program.

2. What is the main idea of paragraph 6?
    a. Claire concluded that alcohol has greatly affected her life.
    b. Claire's mother and father were both alcoholics.
    c. Claire developed her own opinions as she grew older.

3. What is the main idea of paragraph 28?
    a. Claire wanted to become a nurse.
    b. Claire's grades and test scores were not high enough to get into college.
    c. The HEOP program at D'Youville offered Claire, whose grades and test scores had been low, a way into college.

Supporting Details

4. After Claire began first grade, her teacher said
    a. she might need glasses.
    b. she should be transferred to pre-first class.
    c. she should skip directly into second grade.

5. Claire left home and moved in with her friend's family after
    a. her mother caught her breaking curfew.
    b. she was arrested for shoplifting.
    c. her mother moved out of town.

6. Claire's counselor, Mr. DiNardo, helped her by
    a. guiding her into a career-skills program.
    b. suggesting she attend a meeting of a Children of Alcoholics support group.
    c. both of the above.

Conclusions

7. You can conclude from paragraph 10 that
    a. Claire gradually learned she could not depend upon her mother.
    b. Claire does not like to be late for appointments.
    c. Claire's mother never had the money to buy back-to-school clothes.

8. You can conclude from paragraph 12 that
    a. Claire's mother drank quite a lot, but she was not actually an alcoholic.
    b. Claire did not understand the definition of alcoholism.
    c. Claire's mother was unwilling to face the fact that she was an alcoholic.

9. You can conclude from paragraph 26 that
    a. talking with other children of alcoholics helped Claire understand her own situation better.
    b. Mr. DiNardo was once an alcoholic himself.
    c. attending the COA meetings convinced Claire that her mother was not truly an alcoholic.

10. You can conclude from paragraph 29 that
    a. the HEOP program helped Claire develop the skills she needed to succeed in college.
    b. Claire does not believe that she really needed the skills taught by the HEOP program.
    c. students' performances cannot be improved simply by improving their academic background and skills.

SCORE: (Number correct) _____ x 10 = _____ %

Questions for Thinking and Discussion

1. In Claire's dream, educated people eat ravioli while high-school dropouts go hungry. Do you know any dropouts? Are their lives limited by their lack of education? Explain.

2. Claire's mother reacted very angrily when Claire tried to talk to her about her drinking. Why do you think she was so angry? In her own mind, how do you think Claire's mother felt about herself and her drinking?

In the library at D'Youville College, Claire selects a book from the stacks.

3. Claire worked hard to develop the skills needed to do well in college. What specifically can you do to improve your chances for success in school?

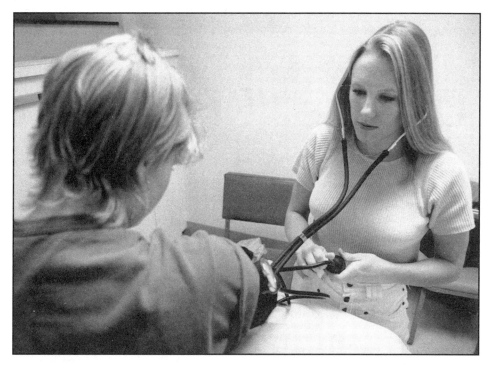

Claire takes the blood pressure of another student in the physical therapy program.

Ideas for Writing

1. Claire drew a lot of strength from meeting with other children of alcoholics. Think of a time you discussed a problem with someone who had experienced a similar problem. Write a paper about your conversation and how the two of you helped each other.

2. Claire improved her skills in the HEOP program, but she probably would have preferred to begin working on them earlier. What are your major study problems? Are your reading skills weak? Do you have trouble managing your time? Choose one major study problem, and write a paper about how it holds you back and what might improve the situation.

His mother was dying, and he was failing school. Using drugs and alcohol to numb his pain, Rick Rivas pretended he didn't care. Once he hit bottom, however, he found the strength to look up. Now, with the support of the people who love him, Rick is making up for lost years.

7 /Enrique "Rick" Rivas

Words to Watch

optimistic (1): very hopeful
The boy was young, so the doctor was *optimistic* that his broken bone would heal quickly.

chaotic (20): out of control; without order
If there were no stop-and-go lights, traffic in the city would be *chaotic*.

outcast (23): someone who has been left out by society
A boy with AIDS is treated like an *outcast* by some students at school.

attentive (24): paying attention
My cat becomes *attentive* when she hears the refrigerator opening.

respirator (31): a machine that provides oxygen to help someone breathe
The patient was too weak to breathe without a *respirator*.

Rick Rivas kneels in front of a vacant lot where drugs are sold.

One day around sunset, our mother started telling us the facts about her health. She spoke in a strong, almost emotionless voice. She was an immigrant from Mexico, a single parent. For someone like her, pain was something you didn't bother with, so for years she had not gone to a doctor. Now she had, but it was too late. The doctors were not optimistic° about her cancer.

It was my freshman year in high school. I lived with my mother and three sisters in San Jose, California. Although I was the only male in the family, I didn't want the role of the "man of the house" and the responsibility that went with it. My sisters and I had never talked much. Now, with Mom sick, we grew further apart than ever.

When I was younger, in junior high, I had stayed away from alcohol and drugs. My sisters were in school with me, and I was afraid that if I drank or took drugs, my mother would find out. But in high school, I began to make up for lost time. I didn't want to be a geek who wouldn't get high.

School became a blur. I'd stumble through the week and then get together with my friends at school on Friday.

"No test for me today. How 'bout you?" one of us would ask.

"Let's go," was usually the answer.

We'd take off to one of their houses

and raid the liquor cabinet. At night I would crawl out my bedroom window and prowl the streets of the cold, misty city with a crew of other restless boys. Night after night I drank. Sometimes it was in a dark church parking lot. Sometimes it was in a friend's back yard. Sometimes it was behind the wheel of my mint-green VW Bug. It didn't matter where, and it didn't matter what. Whether it was beer, wine, or icy-hot peppermint whiskey, I drank heavy, hard, and often.

8   One night I ended up in one of the gang's clubhouses. I had thrown up all over the place. Stumbling out into the night, I stood in the rain. I swallowed the last drops of a bottle of wine and laughed my head off with the realization that I couldn't recall how I had gotten there. Feeling disgusting, I walked home in the morning dew. My mom took one look at me and said, "Take a shower. We're going to church."

9   It's no wonder that in my senior year at Mount Pleasant High, I was reclassified a junior. Instead of beginning school again, I picked up the forms that would allow me to drop out. I remember feeling no guilt in lying to my mother as I gave her the forms to sign.

10   "It's a field trip, Mom," I told her in Spanish. "Sign on the line so I can go."

11   She could speak only a little broken English. I knew she couldn't understand the form. She signed.

12   With school out of the way, I began working the day shift at a pizza parlor. At night I ran with an older, faster crowd. Through them, I was introduced to the love of my life at the time, marijuana. Soon I began to play with the big boys: cocaine, crack, LSD. But grass was always there.

13   It seemed great to be on pot. I could smoke throughout the day, but with cologne, gum, and eye drops to hide what I was doing, who was the wiser? When I wasn't working, I was on a mad hunt for drugs. I was a daily visitor to a guy named Doc. He lived in a run-down neighborhood with thirty Chihuahuas. Flies were thick in the house. I'd wait for him on his front porch while he got my stuff.

14   Staying high became more and more important because my life seemed to be getting steadily worse when I was straight. My mother had deteriorated a great deal. She was like a living skeleton. And when I wasn't high, I was driven crazy by a voice inside my head. Especially when I was alone, it talked to me. It told me over and over that I wasn't worth much, that I wasn't smart, that I never could have made it in school. When I would try to talk back to it, to say that I was worth something, its answer was always the same: "Oh, just go down to Doc's and buy some pot." I always obeyed.

15   One night at work, someone said, "I got acid." I was trying to close out the cash register, but I was already so high I couldn't do the simplest math. My girlfriend finally had to finish the job. I took the acid, turned off the lights, and we left the restaurant. In my foggy state of mind, I didn't notice I had left a beer bottle on the floor.

16   The LSD took effect as we drove around. When I arrived home, around four in the morning, it had not even begun to wear off. I felt panicky. I knew the voice would come back. I lay down and tried to go to sleep, but it was no good. I felt as if I had no flesh, just meat and bones under the blanket. To reassure myself, I got up and stared at myself in the mirror.

17   The next morning at around ten, my boss called. "Rick," he said, "I want you to turn in your uniform."

18   He had found the beer bottle. I had no response. I knew my life was going nowhere, but I was indifferent to the passing of time as long as I had something to smoke or swallow. Somehow I was able to

land a job working at a printed circuit board manufacturing plant. I worked in a high-risk setting with molten solder and heavy equipment. During my breaks, I sat out by a fence in the back of the parking lot, smoking reefers with the other pot-heads. After work, we would take our hunt for drugs all over San Jose. Sometimes I wouldn't make it to work. Instead, I'd end up in some back alley twenty miles away in Santa Cruz, buying drugs from a stranger.

19   By then, my mother's cancer had greatly worsened. Like some poisonous weed, it spread its roots into every part of her body as if trying to replace her with itself. While it ate her alive, I, her only son, did nothing but add to her misery. Sometimes she would lift the oxygen mask from her mouth and whisper to me, "I never imagined in all my years that one of my children would be like you."

20   What she said didn't matter much to me then. I wasn't me anymore; I was a walking dump site of drugs. Things at home had gotten really chaotic°. My older sisters had gotten married and moved out. Somebody needed to pick up the responsibility of buying food, paying bills, and caring for my mom. I wasn't willing to be the one.

21   So one of my older sisters took over. She did what she could around the house. She also took my mother to the hospital and let the rest of us know what was going on with her.

22   One day, she let me know that my little secret wasn't so secret anymore. "Look at you," she said. "You're so thin. We all know you're doing drugs." I denied it, but she had seen a bag of cocaine in my car's glove compartment. I insisted it wasn't mine, that I was just holding it for somebody. She didn't buy it. "You've got to get away from this, Rick." I refused to listen. When she was around, I would leave the house early and stay out as late as possible so I wouldn't have to hear her truthful words.

23   My wasted days had lasted for three years. I was 20 years old. Most of my high-school friends were halfway through college. I would hear them talking to each other, saying things like, "Did you take so-and-so for English? She's a great teacher." I felt like an outcast°. Their conversations sparked my interest in school. Ignoring the voice in my head that said, "You're Rick! Are you kidding? You can't go to school," I took a college placement test at Evergreen Valley College. I was then able to sign up for basic courses in writing and in math.

24   I signed up for class, all right, but that's about all I did. I arrived in the classroom stoned and unprepared. I had no supplies, not even a pencil. Rarely, if ever, would I show up with a clear mind and attentive° attitude. If there was

homework to do, I put it off. I would get high, and the voice in my head would fill me with negative thoughts: "You're not smart enough. You're a high-school dropout. You can't even write a simple sentence." Soon I proved that the voice was right. I had given school another try and failed again.

25   More months went by. My mother became weaker and weaker. The doctors told us the cancer had gone into her bones. Her life could not last much longer.

26   Early in the morning of Thanksgiving Day, my younger sister and I brushed my mother's teeth and bathed her. She didn't even open her eyes. We laid her on the couch. I remember how quiet it was as I took the turkey out of the oven. I tried to make some conversation, to make it livelier for my sister, not wanting her to be frightened. But when she left the room, I called my other sisters. I asked them to come over right away.

27   The first said, "I'm making food. I'll be over around five."

28   "Really, try to hurry," I said.

29   The other sister replied, "Tony went to play football. He's got the car and I've got the kids."

30   "Well, the minute he gets back, get over here."

31   A restless silence filled the house all day, broken only by the noise of my mother's respirator°. At a quarter past six, when dusk had already set in, the last of my sisters arrived.

32   "Mom's not going to make it," I said to her. She looked at Mom on the couch. The image of the skeleton-thin, silent figure was so devastating that my sister turned away. She hurried into the kitchen where there was all this food, unbelievable amounts of food.

33   When she returned from the kitchen, we all went to my mother's side. I spoke softly to her in Spanish, telling her we were all present. I held her hand and, no more than thirty seconds later, she let out a long breath. The respirator, which had been on twenty-four hours a day for the past two years, was silent.

Rick looks for a book at the college library.

34   Rather than seek the comfort of my family that night, I consoled myself with drugs and alcohol. It was far from the last time, but a struggle had begun within me. I began to realize the devastating effects drugs had had on my life. I began to understand that drugs had led me away from school, from my mother, from my sisters, and from my real self.

35   My mom had always been religious, but I had often said I didn't believe in God. Now my sister made a statement that woke me up. "If you don't believe in God, and if you don't believe there is anything after this life, then Mom's spirit isn't around anymore."

36   The idea that Mom's spirit did not exist was too much for me. I began to pray, asking my mother to forgive me. I prayed to have the strength to quit using drugs. Over the next few months, I began pushing back the negative voice in my head. I argued with it, and I won some of those arguments.

37   I avoided my old drug crowd and signed up for an electronics course at a job center. My drug use now involved only marijuana. I would go three or four days without smoking, but then temptation would get the best of me.

38   I prayed that I would find someone who would help me stay on my new path. Then I met Monique Jannel Garcia, who was studying to be a nurse's assistant at the school. We had our first date on Valentine's Day. As I spent more time with Monique, I had less time and desire to use drugs. She made it clear what she expected of me. "If you do drugs," she told me, "I won't be around you."

39   And she meant it. When I didn't show up for a date once, she came after me. She walked through the house to the back yard and found me smoking pot with a guy. She didn't even hesitate. She just walked up and slapped me in the face.

40   "If this is who you are," she said, "I don't want you near me."

41   As she left, I thought, "What am I going to do—take this the way I take everything else, like an emotionless person?"

42   I dropped the joint and ran after her.

43   By October 12, 1991, the day we were married, my drug use had completely stopped. Although I still was tempted, my love for Monique was stronger.

44   Ten months after we were married, we were blessed with a beautiful, healthy baby girl, whom we named Mariah Elaina Rivas. Marriage and the birth of our daughter gave me a strong reason to be a better provider. I decided to give college another try. This time, I was determined to be an A student, not one who just got by.

45   I'm a student now at Evergreen Valley College and have a grade point average of A-/B+. My sisters and I have established a good relationship, and I know my mother is happy about that. Monique and I are buying our own home in a nice area. I've been working at the same computer circuit board shop now for seven years, and I'm now supervisor of the testing department.

46   Most important of all, I've been drug- and alcohol-free for more than two and one-half years. I am no longer a prisoner to addiction, fears, or mental barriers.

47   There is no way to erase the horrible injustice that I did to my mother. What I can do is try to help people who are a lot like I was, people who have dropped out of high school. I bring them books, take them to school, walk them around campus, and show them how to register. "What subject are you afraid of?" I ask them. "Get that out of the way. Bulldoze that barrier."

48   I want to be a voice of encouragement to them. I want them to hear a voice like the one that is in my head now. It speaks in clear, positive tones, and it says one thing: "You can do it, Enrique!"

Vocabulary Check

1. In which sentence does the word **chaotic** make sense?
   a. The classroom was _____, with students yelling and throwing crayons.
   b. After a tough day, I turn out the lights and take a long _____ bath.
   c. My boss deserves a promotion because of his _____ work.

2. In which sentence does the word **attentive** make sense?
   a. It was _____ of my sister to buy a leather coat when she can't pay her phone bill.
   b. I was daydreaming in class, but I became _____ when the teacher called my name.
   c. The girl was so _____ she fell asleep as soon as her head hit the pillow.

3. In the sentences below, the word **deteriorated** means
   a. improved.
   b. gotten worse.
   c. died.

   "My mother had deteriorated a great deal. She was like a living skeleton." (Paragraph 14)

Rick works on an assignment in the college computer lab.

4. In the sentence below, the words **indifferent to** mean
   a. without interest in.
   b. frightened by.
   c. amused by.

   "I knew that my life was going nowhere, but I was indifferent to the passing of time as long as I had something to smoke or swallow." (Paragraph 18)

5. In the sentence below, the word **consoled** means
   a. promised.
   b. educated.
   c. comforted.

   "Rather than seek the comfort of my family that night, I consoled myself with drugs and alcohol." (Paragraph 34)

SCORE: **(Number correct)** _____ **x 20 =** _____ **%**

Reading Check

Central Point and Main Ideas

1. What is the central point of the selection?
   a. Rick regrets using drugs while his mother was alive and now lives a healthy, useful life.
   b. Rick was not responsible when his mother was alive, as shown by the loss of his job.
   c. At first, Rick did poorly in college, but now he is a good student.

2. What is the main idea of paragraph 13?
   a. Rick bought drugs from a man who lived with thirty dogs.
   b. Rick's life was filled with buying and using drugs.
   c. Rick disguised his pot use with cologne, gum, and eye drops.

3. What is the main idea of paragraph 24?
   a. Rick did not carry supplies to his college classes.
   b. When Rick had homework to do, he would put it off.
   c. Rick's fears and actions caused his failure in college.

Supporting Details

4. Rick's mother signed the form to let Rick drop out of school because
   a. she did not understand what she was signing.
   b. she thought he would be better off working than going to school.
   c. she wanted him to go live with relatives in Mexico.

5. Rick lost his job at the pizza parlor when
   a. he got in a fistfight with a customer.
   b. he stole money out of the cash register.
   c. his boss discovered he had been drinking on the job.

6. When Monique found Rick smoking pot, she
   a. called the police.
   b. slapped him and walked away.
   c. asked him to enter a drug program.

7. Today Rick is
   a. a college student and supervisor in a computer circuit board shop.
   b. the manager of a pizza restaurant.
   c. a drug counselor and law-school student.

Conclusions

8. You can conclude from paragraph 3 that
   a. Rick's sisters took drugs when they were in junior high, but they did not want Rick to take them.
   b. Rick really did take drugs when he was in junior high.
   c. Rick was afraid that if he used drugs, his sisters would tell his mother.

9. You can conclude from paragraph 19 that
   a. Rick feels guilty for not being a comfort to his mother while she was ill.
   b. Rick's mother could have gotten better if she had been in the hospital.
   c. Rick's mother thought he turned out better than she had expected.

10. You can conclude from paragraphs 32 and 33 that
    a. Rick's sister was frightened of Rick.
    b. Rick's sister hurried into the kitchen because she was hungry.
    c. Rick realized that his mother would die that day.

SCORE: (Number correct) _____ x 10 = _____%

Questions for Thinking and Discussion

1. Rick talks about a "voice" in his head that used to tell him he was worthless and stupid. These days, that "voice" tells him that he can accomplish whatever he wants. Why do you think its message has changed?

2. Why do you think Rick turned away from his family while his mother was ill? Have you ever felt like withdrawing from your family when a problem arose? What happened?

3. What does Rick mean when he advises students to "bulldoze" the subjects they are afraid of? Is there anything in your life that you would like to bulldoze? Explain.

Rick goes over a diagram of a circuit board with one of the workers that he supervises.

Posing with Rick are his wife, Monique, and their daughter, Mariah.

Ideas for Writing

1. Rick feels bad about the way he treated his mother while she was alive. Have you ever hurt someone and felt bad about it later? Write a letter to that person. Explain what you did and how you feel about it now, and offer an apology.

2. Write a paper explaining whether you think it was right for Monique to slap Rick in the face. Should she have been more understanding about his drug use? Why or why not?

8 / Mikel Foster

Words to Watch

vow (2): promise; pledge
Now that I see how sick my uncle has become from smoking, I *vow* never to smoke.

passionately (5): with great feeling
The boy is so *passionately* interested in dinosaurs that he has read every dinosaur book in the library.

belligerent (13): eager to fight
When the referee called a foul, *belligerent* fans shouted curses and threats.

seizing (16): taking with force
By *seizing* the car keys, the woman stopped her drunken friend from driving the car.

persisted (17): refused to give up a goal or an effort
I *persisted* with the math homework until I was sure I'd done it right.

Mikel Foster shares a meal with a friend in the campus cafeteria.

When I was a little girl, it seemed as if I spent all my waking hours with my father. If he visited his buddies, went to the store, or took a walk, he took me along. I thought the sun rose and set on him. He was tall, slender, and handsome. In my eyes, he was stronger than any superhero on television. More importantly, he adored me. I was his little girl.

My world changed when I was 3 and my parents separated. My wonderful image of my father changed most of all. I didn't think that when my daddy separated from my mother that he would separate from me as well. But that is exactly what happened. He rarely came to visit my brothers and me, and when he did, the visit was disappointing. He would promise to pick us up to visit the zoo or some other fun place. Yet when the appointed day came around, he was nowhere to be found. I took the disappointment hard. With tears streaming down my cheeks, I'd angrily vow° to never believe him or talk to him again. But moments later, I would be asking God, "Please bless my daddy and help him get his life straightened out." In return I promised God I would be nicer to my little brother Michael, not sleep in church while the minister preached, and put all of my church money in the offering basket instead of saving it for the ice-cream man.

3   Eventually, I began to understand that no prayer would change my father. He would change only if he wanted to change himself. I think my experience with my father taught me something valuable. I realized that since I was in control of no one's life except my own, I should concentrate on taking charge of my own life.

4   My mother provided me with a good example of how to take control of one's life. Instead of worrying about my father's life, she concentrated on her own and that of her children. She went to great lengths to make sure that we had the necessities and desires of our hearts. Watching her work and struggle to provide for us, I knew I could never repay her by becoming a failure. No matter how tough her day was, she made time to hear about what happened in school. She was my biggest fan, and I made sure I got good grades in order to hear her praise.

5   One of the biggest gifts my mother gave me was making me realize the importance of family. When she heard my brothers and me fighting, she was quick to step in. With one hand on her hip and the other pointing at us, she would passionately° remind us, "Friends are going to come and go, but the bond that you share as brothers and sister is stronger than any friendship. No matter what happens, you will always need each other."

6   Although she saw how hurt we were by our father's lies, she would not allow us to speak badly of him. "That's still your father, and you will respect him." As strange as it may sound, I think I learned to be dependable from both my parents. Through their examples, I learned that the true test of a person's character is not what is said, but what is done.

7   When the time arrived for me to begin school, I was excited about becoming a big girl with my own book bag and lunch box. Learning to read, write, and spell were adventures to me.

8   One of the best parts of school was learning about other people's lives. Our schoolbooks, stories I read in library books, and our teachers all provided fascinating information about the many different ways in which people lived. So, when I was in third grade and our school sponsored a "Role Model Day" with many guest speakers, I was excited. Police officers, firefighters, lawyers, pilots, accountants—they would all have interesting stories to tell. Imagine my special excitement when my third-grade class heard the local disc jockey was coming as the major speaker of the day. Deejay Tee was as close to a celebrity as most of us had ever known. My friends and I clustered on the sidewalk, awaiting his arrival. He drove up in a candy-apple-red sports car and walked coolly up the sidewalk towards the school. We gazed at him in awe. His black leather pants were accented by a colorful silk shirt and shiny watch. He glanced at us through his dark shades and gave us a smooth "hello." We girls thought he was the most handsome man alive and practically went into a coma. The boys saw him as the coolest person walking the earth.

9   We sat anxiously in our seats as Deejay Tee appeared on the auditorium stage. I gazed at him adoringly, waiting to hear his assurance that I could become anything I wanted to be. Instead, our local hero gave a speech that shocked and frightened me. In the most serious tones, he told us, "The majority of you sitting here listening to me will not make it. Some of you will turn to a life of crime, violence, and drugs. A few of you will die before you turn 20. Half of you will become parents while you are still in school. Sad as this speech may be, this is the reality of your future."

10   He slowly looked over the audience, and it seemed that he was looking straight at me. I sat terrified, feeling as if those who would and would not make it had been assigned, and I had been chosen as one who wouldn't. The bright sunshine of the day disappeared, and dark clouds took its place.

11   As my shock subsided and I was able to think clearly again, one thought stood out. Deejay Tee was wrong to say those awful things, and I was going to prove it. I promised myself three things that day. First, I was going to make it. Second, if I ever got the chance to stand before third grade students, I would never forecast such gloom and doom for them. And lastly, I would never put anyone on a pedestal and be disappointed again. Although I was only eight years old when I made these promises, they continue to guide my life today. Whenever the pressures of life seem more than I can bear, I reflect back to my promises and my focus is renewed.

12   When it was time to enter middle school, I looked at what lay ahead. The school that my friends and I would be entering sounded bad to me. I heard about the fights and drugs that were part of the daily scene there. I wanted something better, so I managed to transfer to a music school in the district where I could play viola in the school orchestra. In the months and years ahead, I kept track of what happened to students I knew who went to the public middle school. When I did, I saw Deejay Tee's horrid description of our futures becoming reality. Seventh-grade girls were becoming mothers. The numbers increased so fast that having a baby in junior high was the norm. One of my friends had three kids before she finished junior high. Many of the boys sought the fast life. Living in a community where honest money was hard to come by, I wasn't surprised to learn that a friend was dealing drugs. Young kids working as lookouts for drug dealers earned more money than their parents. Many of my friends were in jail. Others were dying violent deaths.

13   Drugs were invading our neighborhood, but nothing prepared me for drugs invading my family. Some of my aunts and uncles became loud and belligerent°. They were unable to sit down when they visited, and they visited only when they needed money. Possessions started disappearing from our house. I hated what was happening in the community, but I hated more what was happening to my family.

14   As if all this were not enough, drive-by shootings were happening everywhere. Some of my classmates were victims. Now I was really scared. I could say no to drugs, crime, and teenage pregnancy, but how could I avoid being killed by a stray

bullet? No matter how much of a "good girl" I was, I could still be the victim of a bullet intended for someone else. When this was my reality, how could I expect more out of life?

15   Somehow, I did manage to expect more. I couldn't deny the hard reality of the cards that had been dealt me, but I wasn't about to give up hope. Others around me might have accepted Deejay Tee's horrible prophecy for their lives, but that didn't mean I had to do so. I prayed each time I left my home and gave thanks each time I reached my destination safely. Each new day, I felt a step closer to the success I knew was around the corner.

16   Throughout high school, the problems that had begun in middle school became even more serious. More and more of my classmates dropped by the wayside, becoming statistics lost to drugs, crime, and teenage parenthood. I concentrated harder on my academics, on involvement in clubs, on volunteering time in a health clinic. My efforts paid off. By seizing° control of my life, I graduated in the top 10 percent of my class and was on the pathway of success. I was accepted at High Point University in North Carolina.

17   College acceptance was not the end of my struggles. I had earned a partial scholarship and some other financial aid, but I was still several thousand dollars short of what I needed to enroll. Every door I approached seemed tightly closed. My mother's money had been used up getting my older brother through college. But I spoke to friends, relatives, anyone I

thought could help me. I persisted° until I received a work-study grant from the same financial-aid office that had said nothing could be done. I was now a fully enrolled freshman majoring in sports medicine and earning a B+ average.

Mikel reacts to a point made in a classroom discussion.

18   I know that all my obstacles are not behind me. A missed assignment, financial-aid problems, homesickness, illness, discrimination, or a change in career choice may make me stumble on my path. But I am ready to confront whatever happens. Deejay Tee was not looking at me that day he spoke at our school. I am in control of my life.

Vocabulary Check

1. In which sentence would the word **belligerent** make sense?
   a. The _____ neighbor smiled and waved as we drove past his house.
   b. The shopper was _____ when she found out that the shirt she liked was on sale.
   c. When the cashier told him the register was closed after he had waited in line for forty-five minutes, the man became _____.

2. In the sentence below, the word **bond** means
   a. meals.
   b. money.
   c. connection.

   ". . . she would passionately remind us, 'Friends are going to come and go, but the bond that you share as brothers and sister is stronger than any friendship.'" (Paragraph 5)

3. In the sentence below, the word **subsided** means
   a. worsened.
   b. became less.
   c. grew.

   "As my shock subsided and I was able to think clearly again, one thought stood out." (Paragraph 11)

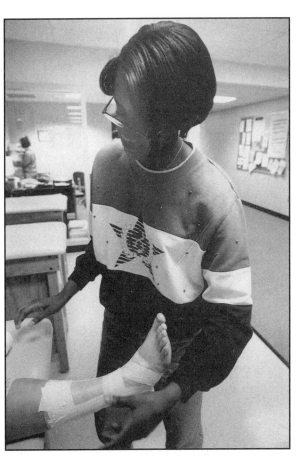

Majoring in sports medicine, Mikel learns the correct way to tape a sprained ankle.

4. In the sentence below, the word **prophecy** means
   a. prediction.
   b. policy.
   c. mystery.

   "Others around me might have accepted Deejay Tee's horrible prophecy for their lives, but that didn't mean I had to do so." (Paragraph 15)

5. In the sentences below, the word **obstacles** means
   a. things that stand in the way.
   b. assignments.
   c. a variety of choices.

   "I know that all my obstacles are not behind me. A missed assignment, financial-aid problems, homesickness, illness, discrimination, or a change in career choice may make me stumble on my path." (Paragraph 18)

SCORE: **(Number correct)** _____ x 20 = _____%

Reading Check

Central Point and Main Ideas

1. What is the central point of the selection?
   a. All children need heroes, and Mikel and her friends found theirs in Deejay Tee.
   b. After his divorce, Mikel's father was irresponsible in his treatment of his children.
   c. Taking control of her life, Mikel rose above Deejay Tee's vision of an awful future.

2. What is the main idea of paragraph 4?
   a. Mikel's mother was a good example and inspiration for Mikel.
   b. Mikel's mother worked very hard.
   c. Mikel's mother did not care what happened to her former husband.

3. What is the main idea of paragraph 11?
   a. After Deejay Tee's speech, Mikel got over her shock.
   b. Deejay Tee's speech caused Mikel to make some important decisions.
   c. Sometimes Mikel experiences great pressures.

4. What is the main idea of paragraph 17?
   a. Mikel's struggles did not end when she was accepted at college.
   b. Mikel received a grant that helped her enroll in college, where she is doing very well with a sports medicine major.
   c. Mikel's mother spent her savings sending her older brother through college.

Supporting Details

5. When her parents first separated, Mikel thought she could make her father get his life in order by
   a. telling him how much she needed him.
   b. taking him to the zoo or other fun places.
   c. being nicer to her brother and behaving in church.

6. When Mikel first saw Deejay Tee, she felt that
   a. he was the most handsome man alive.
   b. he had kept the audience waiting too long.
   c. his colorful silk shirt and black leather pants looked silly.

7. After listening to Deejay Tee's speech, Mikel thought that
   a. he was wrong to speak about such terrible possibilities to young children.
   b. the speech dealt accurately with topics that kids should think about.
   c. his speech was too long and boring.

8. Deejay Tee's prediction about drugs, crime and pregnancy turned out to be
   a. false because those problems never affected Mikel or her classmates.
   b. true because Mikel began using drugs with her classmates.
   c. true for many people in Mikel's life but not for her.

Conclusions

9. You can conclude from paragraph 13 that
   a. Mikel enjoyed visits from her noisy aunts and uncles.
   b. some of Mikel's relatives were stealing her family's possessions to buy drugs.
   c. like Mikel's aunts and uncles, Mikel's mother starting taking drugs.

10. You can conclude from paragraph 15 that
    a. Mikel could not ignore the forces working against her, but she did not allow them to stop her from reaching her goals.
    b. Mikel was a skilled card player who almost always won.
    c. like many of her classmates, Mikel had accepted Deejay Tee's terrible prophecy.

SCORE: (Number correct) _____ x 10 = _____ %

Mikel uses a computer as part of her work-study job at High Point University.

Mikel spends some quiet moments in the university chapel.

Questions for Thinking and Discussion

1. How do you think Mikel Foster managed to avoid the problems that many of her classmates had? What positive forces were there in her life that some of her classmates may have lacked?

2. Have you, like Mikel, ever been angered by someone's low opinion of you? Did you do anything to show this person that he or she was wrong? Explain.

3. Mikel writes that "the true test of a person's character is not what is said, but what is done." What does she mean by this? Do you agree with her statement? Why or why not?

Ideas for Writing

1. Mikel kept herself busy by studying hard, joining clubs, and volunteering her time. Those activities helped her stay out of trouble and get into a university. Think of an activity or hobby that you enjoy. Write a paper describing the activity. Tell what you get out of it now and how you think it could benefit you in the future.

2. Mikel thinks that Deejay Tee was wrong to say what he did. But she also says that his words encouraged her to do her best. Write a paper explaining whether you think he was right or wrong to say what he did to the schoolchildren.

From the age of 14 on, Joe Davis followed a path that led him closer and closer to self-destruction. He lived in a world of drugs, guns, and money. In this world, he had no respect for himself or sympathy for others. Today Joe Davis is, in every way, a new man. Here is the story of how Joe saved his own life.

9 / Joe Davis

Words to Watch

option (6): choice
Most public school students have the *option* of either bringing lunch or eating in the cafeteria.

encountered (20): met
My father was amazed when he *encountered* a man who looked just like him.

absolutely (20): completely; totally
The rumor about the minister was *absolutely* untrue.

unruly (26): badly behaved
After an hour passed and the concert did not begin, the audience became *unruly*.

hushed (27): quiet
The ticking of the clock was the only sound in the *hushed*, empty house.

Joe Davis tells students his story.

Joe Davis was the coolest 14-year-old he'd ever seen. 1

He went to school when he felt like it. He hung out with a wild crowd. He started drinking some wine, smoking some marijuana. "Nobody could tell me anything," he says today. "I thought the sun rose and set on me." There were rules at home, and Joe didn't do rules. So he moved in with his grandmother. 2

Joe Davis was the coolest 16-year-old he'd ever seen. 3

Joe's parents gave up on his schooling and signed him out of the tenth grade. Joe went to work in his dad's body shop, but that didn't last long. There were rules there, too, and Joe didn't do rules. By the time he was in his mid-teens, Joe was taking pills that got him high and even using cocaine. He was also smoking marijuana all the time and drinking booze all the time. 4

Joe Davis was the coolest 25-year-old he'd ever seen. 5

He was living with a woman almost twice his age. The situation wasn't great, but she paid the bills, and certainly Joe couldn't. He had his habit to support, which by now had grown to include heroin. Sometimes he'd work at a low-level job, if someone else found it for him. He might work long enough to get a paycheck and 6 then spend it all at once. Other times he'd be caught stealing and get fired first. A more challenging job was not an option°, even if he had bothered to look for one. He couldn't put words together to form a sentence, unless the sentence was about drugs. Filling out an application was difficult. He wasn't a strong reader. He couldn't do much with numbers. Since his drug habit had to be paid for, he started to steal. First he stole from his parents, then from his sister. Then he stole from the families of people he knew. But eventually the people he knew wouldn't let him in their houses since they knew he'd steal from them. So he got a gun and began holding people up. He chose elderly people and others who weren't likely to fight back. The holdups kept him in drug money, but things at home were getting worse. His woman's teenage daughter was getting out of line. Joe decided it was up to him to discipline her. The girl didn't like it. She told her boyfriend. One day, the boyfriend called Joe out of the house.

7   BANG.

8   Joe Davis was in the street, his nose in the dirt. His mind was still cloudy from his most recent high, but he knew something was terribly wrong with his legs. He couldn't move them; he couldn't even feel them. His mother came out of her nearby house and ran to him. As he heard her screams, he imagined what she was seeing. Her oldest child, her first baby, her bright boy who could have been and done anything, was lying in the gutter, a junkie with a .22 caliber bullet lodged in his spine.

9   The next time Joe's head cleared, he was in a hospital bed, blinking up at his parents as they stared helplessly at him. The doctors had done all they could; Joe would live, to everyone's surprise. But he was a paraplegic—paralyzed from his chest on down. It was done. It was over. It was written in stone. He would not walk again. He would not be able to control his bladder or bowels. He would not be able to make love as he had before. He would not be able to hold people up, then hurry away.

Joe spent the next eight months   10 being moved between several Philadelphia hospitals, where he was shown the ropes of life as a paraplegic. Officially he was being "rehabilitated"—restored to a productive life. There was just one problem: Joe. "To be *re*habilitated, you must have been *habilitated* first," he says today. "That wasn't me." During his stay in the hospitals, he found ways to get high every day.

Finally Joe was released from the   11 hospital. He returned in his wheelchair to the house he'd been living in when he was shot. He needed someone to take care of him, and his woman friend was still willing. His drug habit was as strong as ever, but his days as a stick-up man were over. So he started selling drugs. Business was good. The money came in fast, and his own drug use accelerated even faster.

12   A wheelchair-bound junkie doesn't pay much attention to his health and cleanliness. Eventually Joe developed his first bedsore: a deep, rotting wound that ate into his flesh, overwhelming him with its foul odor. He was admitted to Magee Rehabilitation Hospital, where he spent six months on his stomach while the ghastly wound slowly healed. Again, he spent his time in the hospital using drugs. This time his drug use did not go unnoticed. Soon before he was scheduled to be discharged, hospital officials kicked him out. He returned to his friend's house and his business. But then police raided the house. They took the drugs, they took the money, they took the guns.

13   "I really went downhill then," says Joe. With no drugs and no money to get drugs, life held little meaning. He began fighting with the woman he was living with. "When you're in the state I was in, you don't know how to be nice to anybody," he says. Finally she kicked him out of the house. When his parents took him in, Joe did a little selling from their house, trying to keep it low-key, out of sight, so they wouldn't notice. He laughs at the notion today. "I thought I could control junkies and tell them 'Business only during certain hours.'" Joe got high when his monthly Social Security check came, high when he'd make a purchase for someone else and get a little something for himself, high when a visitor would share drugs with him. It wasn't much of a life. "There I was," he says, "a junkie with no education, no job, no friends, no means of supporting myself. And now I had a spinal cord injury."

14   Then came October 25, 1988. Joe had just filled a prescription for pills to con-

trol his muscle spasms. Three hundred of the powerful muscle relaxants were there for the taking. He swallowed them all.

15   "It wasn't the spinal cord injury that did it," he says. "It was the addiction."

16   Joe tried hard to die, but it didn't work. A sister heard him choking and called for help. He was rushed to the hospital, where he lay in a coma for four days.

17   Joe has trouble finding the words to describe what happened next.

18   "I had . . . a spiritual awakening, for lack of any better term," he says. "My soul had been cleansed. I knew my life could be better. And from that day to this, I have chosen not to get high."

19   Drugs, he says, "are not even a temptation. That life is a thing that happened to someone else."

20   Joe knew he wanted to turn himself around, but he needed help in knowing where to start. He enrolled in Magee Hospital's vocational rehabilitation program. For six weeks, he immersed himself in discussions, tests, and exercises to help him determine the kind of work he might be suited for. The day he finished the rehab program, a nurse at Magee told him about a receptionist's job in the spinal cord injury unit at Thomas Jefferson Hospital. He went straight to the hospital and met Lorraine Buchanan, coordinator of the unit. "I told her where I was and where I wanted to go," Joe says. "I told her, 'If you give me a job, I will never disappoint you. I'll quit first if I see I can't live up to it.'" She gave him the job. The wheelchair-bound junkie, the man who'd never been able to hold a job, the drug-dependent stickup man who "couldn't put two words together to make a sentence" was now the first face, the first voice that patients encountered° when they entered the spinal cord unit. "I'd never talked to people like that," says Joe, shaking his head. "I had absolutely°

no background. But Lorraine and the others, they taught me to speak. Taught me to greet people. Taught me to handle the phone." How did he do in his role as a receptionist? A huge smile breaks across Joe's face as he answers, "I did excellent."

21   A month after Joe started his job, another new chapter began in his life. He was riding a city bus to work. A woman recovering from knee surgery was in another seat. The two smiled, but didn't speak.

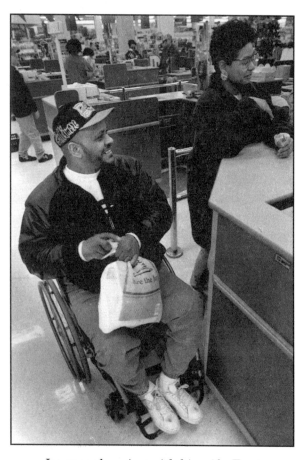

Joe goes shopping with his wife, Terri.

22   A week later, Joe spotted the woman again. The bus driver sensed something was going on and encouraged Joe to approach her. Her name was Terri. She was a receptionist in a law office. On their first date, Joe laid his cards on the table. He told her his story. He also told her he was looking to get married. "That about scared her away," Joe recalls. "She

said she wasn't interested in marriage. I asked, 'Well, suppose you did meet someone you cared about, who cared about you, and treated you well. Would you still be opposed to the idea of marriage?' She said no, she would consider it then. I said, 'Well, that's all I ask.'"

23   Four months later, as the two sat over dinner in a restaurant, Joe handed Terri a box tied with a ribbon. Inside was a smaller box. Then a smaller box, and a smaller one still. Ten boxes in all. Inside the smallest was an engagement ring. After another six months, the two were married in the law office where Terri works. Since then, she has been Joe's constant source of support, encouragement, and love.

24   After Joe had started work at Jefferson Hospital, he talked with his supervisor, Lorraine, about his dreams of moving on to something bigger, more challenging. She encouraged him to try college. He had taken and passed the high-school general equivalency diploma (GED) exam years before, almost as a joke, when he was recovering from his bedsore at Magee. Now he enrolled in a university mathematics course. He didn't do well. "I wasn't ready," Joe says. "I'd been out of school seventeen years. I dropped out." Before he could let discouragement overwhelm him, he enrolled at Community College of Philadelphia (CCP), where he signed up for basic math and English courses. He worked hard, sharpening study skills he had never developed in his earlier school days. Next he took courses towards an associate's degree in mental health and social services, along with a certificate in addiction studies. Five years later, he graduated from CCP, the first member of his family ever to earn a college degree.

25   Now Joe is a student at Hahnemann University in Philadelphia, working towards a bachelor's degree in mental health. He hopes eventually to earn a

master's degree in social work. He's moved from his receptionist's job at Jefferson Hospital to unit desk clerk at Magee Hospital, where he had recovered from his shooting fourteen years ago. His dream now is to get into the "real world," the world of young men and women immersed in drugs, violence, and crime. Whenever he can, he speaks at local schools through a program called Think First. He tells young people about his drug use, his shooting, and his experience with paralysis.

26   At a presentation at a disciplinary school outside of Philadelphia, Joe gazes with quiet authority at the unruly° crowd of teenagers. He begins to speak, telling them about speedballs and guns, fast money and bedsores, even about the leg bag that collects his urine. At first, the kids snort with laughter at his honesty. When they laugh, he waits patiently, then goes on. Gradually the room grows quieter as Joe tells them of his life and then asks them about theirs. "What's important to you? What are your goals?" he says. "I'm nearly 40 years old and still in school because when I was young, I chose the dead-end route many of you are on. But now I'm doing what I have to do to get where I want to go. What are *you* doing?"

27   He tells them more, about broken dreams, about his parents' grief, about the former friends who turned away from him when he was no longer a source of drugs. He tells them of the continuing struggle to regain the trust of people he once abused. He tells them about the desire that consumes him now, the desire to make his community a better place to live. His wish is that no young man or woman should have to walk the path he's walked in order to value the precious gift of life. The teenagers are now silent. They look at this broad-shouldered black man in his wheelchair, his head and beard close-shaven, a gold ring in his ear. His hushed° words settle among them like gentle drops of cleansing rain. "What are *you* doing? Where are *you* going?" he asks them. "Think about it. Think about me."

28   Joe Davis is the coolest 39-year-old you've ever seen.

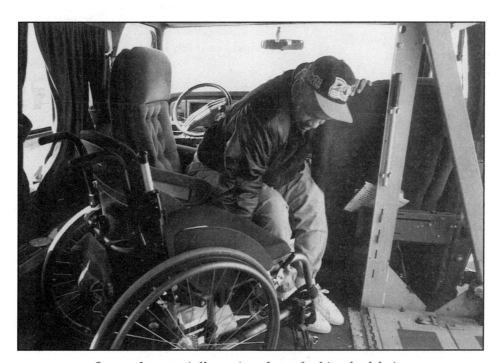

Joe needs a specially equipped van for his wheelchair.

Vocabulary Check

1. In which sentence would the word **option** make sense?
   a. The students learned a valuable _____ by taking part in the science fair.
   b. I'd like you to do me a favor, but you have the _____ of saying no.
   c. Anyone with an _____ will get a free bottle of soda at the supermarket.

2. In which sentence would the word **encountered** make sense?
   a. In my dream, I _____ an alien from outer space.
   b. The movie was so poor that we _____ it after just half an hour.
   c. The girl _____ her friends a funny story about her baby brother.

3. In the sentence below, the word **restored** means
   a. held back.
   b. punished.
   c. brought back.

   "Officially he was being 'rehabilitated'— restored to a productive life." (Paragraph 10)

Joe asks students to think about their life choices.

4. In the sentence below, the word **accelerated** means
   a. increased.
   b. grew less serious.
   c. disappeared.

   "The money came in fast, and his own drug use accelerated even faster." (Paragraph 11)

5. In the sentence below, the word **immersed** means
   a. totally ignored.
   b. greatly angered.
   c. deeply involved.

   "For six weeks, he immersed himself in discussions, tests, and exercises to help him determine the kind of work he might be suited for." (Paragraph 20)

SCORE: (Number correct) _____ x 20 = _____%

Reading Check

Central Point and Main Ideas

1. What is the central point of the reading?
   a. Most people cannot improve their lives once they turn to drugs and crime.
   b. Joe Davis overcame a life of drugs and crime and a disability to lead a rich, productive life.
   c. The rules of Joe Davis's parents caused him to leave home and continue a life of drugs and crime.

2. What is the main point of paragraph 9?
   a. Joe still had the ability to move his arms.
   b. Joe's paralysis changed his life in many ways.
   c. After he was shot, Joe could no longer hold people up.

3. What is the main idea of paragraph 24?
   a. It was difficult for Joe to do college work after being out of school for many years.
   b. Lorraine Buchanan encouraged Joe to go to college.
   c. Joe overcame a lack of academic preparation and eventually succeeded in college.

Supporting Details

4. Joe Davis quit high school
   a. when he was 14.
   b. when he got a good job at a hospital.
   c. when he was in tenth grade.

5. Joe tried to kill himself by
   a. swallowing muscle relaxant pills.
   b. shooting himself.
   c. overdosing on heroin.

6. How did Joe meet his future wife?
   a. She was a nurse in the hospital where he recovered from the shooting.
   b. She was a patient in the spinal cord injury unit where he worked as a receptionist.
   c. She and Joe were passengers on the same city bus.

7. Joe decided to stop using drugs
   a. when he met Terri.
   b. when he was shot.
   c. when he awoke from his suicide attempt.

Conclusions

8. You can conclude from paragraph 2 that
   a. Joe's grandmother was less strict than his parents.
   b. Joe's friends disapproved of his drinking.
   c. Joe's parents did not try to control their son.

9. You can conclude from paragraph 25 that
   a. Joe finds it easy to go to school, work, and speak for Think First.
   b. Joe strongly disliked his job at Thomas Jefferson Hospital.
   c. Joe wants to use his past mistakes to help others.

10. You can conclude from paragraph 26 that
    a. Joe will reveal very personal information about himself in order to reach young people with his story.
    b. Joe was angry at the Philadelphia students who laughed at parts of his story.
    c. Joe is glad he waited until he was nearly 40 to attend college.

SCORE: (Number correct) _____ x 10 = _____%

Questions for Thinking and Discussion

1. If you had been one of the people Joe robbed before he was paralyzed, how would you have felt about him? Do you think reading this story would in any way change your feelings about him?

2. Why do you think the Philadelphia students laughed at Joe's honesty? Why do you think they became quieter as he continued to tell them about his life? What effect do you think his presentation has on students?

3. Joe Davis wants young people to learn the lessons he did without having to repeat his hard experiences. What lesson have you learned that you would like to pass on to a friend or family member who is younger than you?

Ideas for Writing

1. If you met Joe Davis, what would you like to say to him? Write him a letter telling him how you feel about his story. If you think you will remember his story, explain why. Include any questions you would like to ask him.

2. Joe's parents loved him, but they weren't able to keep him from taking drugs. Think about a situation in which young people can run into trouble. Then write a paper explaining what steps you think parents or other adults could take to help them.

10 / Maria Cardenas

Words to Watch

enraged (13): angered
I was *enraged* by the men's mistreatment of the stray dog.

abducted (17) taken away by force
During World War II, many Jewish people were *abducted* from their homes and sent to death camps.

taunted (21): cruelly teased
Some children in class *taunted* the new student about her accent.

mandatory (24): required by law
School attendance is *mandatory* until age 16.

eligible (24): qualified
My sister's high grades made her *eligible* to win a scholarship.

Maria Cardenas listens and takes notes in class.

As I walk into the classroom, the teacher gazes at me with her piercing green eyes. I feel myself shrinking and burning up with guilt. I go straight to her desk and hand her the excuse slip. Just like all the other times, I say, "I was sick." I hate lying, but I have to. I don't want my parents to get in trouble. 1

I'm not a very good liar. She makes me hold out my hands, inspecting my dirty fingernails and calluses. She knows exactly where I've been the past several days. When you pick tomatoes and don't wear gloves, your hands get rough and stained from the plant oils. Soap doesn't wash that out. 2

In the background, I can hear the students giggling as she asks her usual questions: "What was wrong? Was your brother sick, too? Do you feel better today?" Of course I don't feel better. My whole body aches from those endless hot days spent harvesting crops from dawn to dusk. I was never absent by choice. 3

That year, in that school, I think my name was "Patricia Rodriguez," but I'm not sure. My brother and I used whatever name our mother told us to use each time we went to a new school. We understood that we had to be registered as the children of parents who were in the United States legally, in case Immigration ever checked up. 4

5   My parents had come to the States in the late '60s to work in the fields and earn money to feed their family. They paid eight hundred dollars to someone who smuggled them across the border, and they left us with our aunt and uncle in Mexico. My five-year-old brother, Joel, was the oldest. I was 4, and then came Teresa, age 3, and baby Bruno. The other kids in the neighborhood teased us, saying, "They won't come back for you." Three years later, our parents sent for us to join them in Texas. My little heart sang as we waved good-bye to those neighbor kids in Rio Verde. My father did love us!

6   My parents worked all the time in the fields. Few other options were open to them because they had little education. Our education was important to them. They were too scared to put us in school the first year, but when I was 8 they did enroll us. I do remember that my first-grade report card said I was "Antonietta Gonzales." My father always made sure we had everything we needed—tablets, crayons, ruler, and the little box to put your stuff in. He bragged to his friends about his children going to school. Now we could talk for our parents. We could translate their words for the grocer, the doctor, and the teachers. If Immigration came by, we could tell them we were citizens, and because we were speaking English, they wouldn't ask any more questions.

7   In the years to come, I often reminded myself that my father had not forgotten us like the fathers of so many kids I knew. It became more important for me to remember that as it became harder to see that he loved us. He had hit my mother once in a while as I was growing up, but when his own mother died in Mexico in 1973, his behavior grew much worse. My uncles told me that my father, the youngest of the family, had often beaten his mother. Maybe it was the guilt he felt when she died, but for whatever reason, he started drinking heavily, abusing my mother emotionally and physically, and terrorizing us kids. The importance of our education faded away, and now my papa thought my brother and I should work more in the fields. We would work all the time—on school vacations, holidays, weekends, and every day after school. When there were lots of tomatoes to pick, I went to school only every other day.

8   If picking was slow, I stayed home after school and cooked for the family. I started as soon as I got home in the afternoon. I used the three large pots my mother owned: one for beans, one for rice or soup, and one for hot salsa. There were also the usual ten pounds of flour or *maseca*, ground corn meal, for the tortillas. I loved this cooking because I could eat as much as I wanted and see that the

little kids got enough before the older family members finished everything. By this time there were three more children in our family, and we often went to bed hungry. (My best subject in school was lunch, and my plate was always clean.)

9   Life was never easy in those days. Traveling with the harvest meant living wherever the bosses put us. We might be in little houses with one outdoor toilet for the whole camp. Other times the whole crew, all fifty or one hundred of us, were jammed into one big house. Working in the fields meant blistering sun, aching muscles, sliced fingers, bug bites, and my father yelling when we didn't pick fast enough to suit him. But we were kids, so we found a way to have some fun. My brother and I would make a game of competing with each other and the other adults. I never did manage to pick more than Joel, but I came close. One time I picked 110 baskets of cucumbers to Joel's 115. We made thirty-five cents a basket.

10   Of course, we never saw any of that money. At the end of the week, whatever the whole family had earned was given to my father. Soon he stopped working altogether. He just watched us, chatted with the field bosses, and drank beer. He began to beat all of us kids as well as our mother. We didn't work fast enough for him. He wanted us to make more money. He called us names and threw stones and vegetables at us. The other workers did nothing to make him stop. I was always scared of my father, but I loved him even though he treated us so badly. I told myself that he loved us, but that alcohol ruled his life.

11   I knew what controlled my father's life, but I never thought about being in control of my own. I did as I was told, spoke in a whisper, and tried not to be noticed. Because we traveled with the harvest, my brothers and sisters and I attended three or four different schools in one year. When picking was good, I went to the fields instead of school. When the little kids got sick, I stayed home to watch them. When I did go to school, I didn't understand very much. I don't know how I got through elementary school, much less to high school, because I only knew how to add, subtract, and multiply. And let's just say I got "introduced" to English writing skills and grammar.

12   In 1978, my mother ran away after two weeks of terrible beatings. Joel and I found the dime under the big suitcase, where she had told us it would be. We were supposed to use it to call the police, but we were too scared. We stayed in the upstairs closet with our brothers and sisters. In the morning, I felt guilty and terrified. I didn't know whether our mother was alive or dead. Not knowing what else to do, I got dressed and went to school. I told the counselor what had happened, and she called the police. My father was arrested. He believed the police when they said they were taking him to jail for unpaid traffic tickets. Then the police located my mother and told her it was safe to come out of hiding. My father never lived with us again although he continued to stalk us. He would stand outside the house yelling at my mother, "You're gonna be a prostitute. Those kids are gonna be no-good drug addicts and criminals. They're gonna end up in jail."

13   My father's words enraged° me. I had always had a hunger for knowledge, always dreamed of a fancy job where I would go to work wearing nice clothes and carrying a briefcase. How dare he try to kill my dream! True, the idea of that dream ever coming true seemed unlikely. In school, I would ask about material I didn't understand, but most of the teachers seemed annoyed at my interruptions. My mother would warn me, "Please, don't ask so many questions." Eventually I got discouraged and sat quietly in my classrooms, almost invisible.

14   But then, somehow, when I was 14, Mrs. Mercer noticed me. I don't remember how my conversations with this teacher started, but it led to her offering me a job in the Western clothing store she and her husband owned. I helped translate for the Spanish-speaking customers who shopped there. I worked only Saturdays, and I got paid a whole twenty-dollar bill. Proudly, I presented that money to my mother. The thought "I can actually do more than field work" began to make my dreams seem like possibilities. I began to believe I could be something more.

15   The month of my sixteenth birthday, Mrs. Mercer recommended me for a cashier's job in the local supermarket. I worked there for six weeks, and on Friday, January 16, 1981, I was promoted to head cashier. I was on top of the world! I could not believe such good things were happening to me. I had a good job, and I was on my way to becoming my school's first Spanish-speaking graduate. I thought nothing could go wrong, ever again. But that very night, my dreams were shattered again—this time, I thought, permanently.

16   The manager let me off at nine, two hours early. I didn't have a ride because my brother was not picking me up until 11:00 p.m. But I was in luck! I saw a man I knew, a friend of my brother's, someone I had worked with in the fields. He was a trusted family friend, so when he offered me a lift, I said, "Of course." Now I could go home and tell everybody about the promotion.

17   I never made it home or to my big promotion. The car doors were locked; I could not escape. I was abducted° and raped, and I found myself walking down the same abusive road as my mother. My dreams were crushed. I had failed. In my old-fashioned Mexican world, I was a "married woman," even if I wasn't. To go home again would have been to dishonor my family. When I found I was pregnant, there seemed to be only one path open to me. I married my abductor, dropped out of school, and moved with him to Oklahoma.

One of Maria's seasonal farm jobs is picking oranges in Florida.

18   "My father was right," I thought. "I am a failure." But dreams die hard. My brother Joel was living in the same Oklahoma town as I was. He would see me around town, my face and body bruised from my husband's beatings. But unlike the workers in the fields who had silently watched our father's abuse, Joel spoke up. "You've got to go," he would urge me. "You don't have to take this. Go on, you can make it."

19   "No!" I would tell him. I was embarrassed to have anyone know what my life had become. I imagined returning to my mother, only to have to have her repri-

mand me, saying, "What's the matter with you that you can't even stay married?"

20   But Joel wouldn't give up. Finally he told me, "I don't care what you say. I am going to tell Mother what is going on."

21   And he did. He explained to our mother that I had been forced to go with that man, that I was being abused, and that I was coming home. She accepted what he told her. I took my little girl and the clothes I could carry, threw everything into my car, and left Oklahoma for Florida. My husband taunted° me just as my father had my mother: "You'll be on food stamps! You can't amount to anything on your own!" But I proved him wrong. I worked days in the fields and nights as a cashier, getting off work at midnight and up early the next day to work again. I don't know how I did it, but I kept up the payments on my little car, I earned my high-school general equivalency diploma (GED), I didn't go on food stamps, and I was happy.

22   The years passed, and I married a wonderful man who loved me and my daughter. He was proud that I had some real education, and he knew that I wanted more. But I couldn't imagine that going on in school was possible.

23   Then, in 1987, I was working for the Redlands Christian Migrant Association. They provided services for migrant children. One day, in the office, I picked up a book called *Dark Harvest*. It was filled with stories about migrant workers. I had never read a book before, but this one was about people like me. I began reading it, slowly at first, then with more and more interest. Some of the people in it had gone back for a GED, just as I had! Even more—some had gone on to college and earned a degree in education. Now they were teaching. When I read that book, I realized that my dream wasn't crazy. I finally knew what I wanted to do.

24   My husband and I took the mandatory° steps to become legally admitted residents of the United States. Then, my husband found out about a federal program that helps seasonal farm workers go to college. I applied and found I was eligible°. When I took my diagnostic tests, my reading, English, and math levels turned out to be seventh-grade level. Not as bad as I thought! The recruiter asked if I would mind attending Adult Basic Education classes to raise my scores to the twelfth-grade level. Mind? I was thrilled! I loved to study, and in spite of a serious illness that kept me out of classes for weeks, my teacher thought I was ready to try the ABE exams early. Her encouragement gave my confidence a boost, and I found my scores had zoomed up to a 12.9 level.

25   Then, in the fall of 1994, I took the greatest step of my academic life. Proud and excited, I started classes at Edison Community College in Florida. Of course, I was also terrified, trembling inside almost like that scared little girl who used to tiptoe up to the teacher's desk with her phony absence excuses. But I'm not a scared little kid anymore. My self-confidence is growing, even if it's growing slowly. I have a hard-working husband and three children, all of whom I love very much. I look at my 13-year-old, Antonietta, who began to travel with us to pick blueberries last summer. She works in the fields, as I did, but there is little resemblance between her life and mine. She and our other children are in one school the whole year long. Antonietta works at her own pace, learning the value of work and of money—and she keeps what she earns. Already, her teachers are beginning to encourage her to become a journalist because of her skill in writing.

26   And guess what! My teachers compliment my writing too. When I enrolled in my developmental English class at Edison, my teacher, Johanna Seth, asked

the class to write a narrative paragraph. A narrative, she explained, tells a story. As I thought about what story I could write, a picture of a scared little girl in a schoolroom popped into my head. I began writing:

> *As I walk into the classroom, the teacher gazes at me with her piercing green eyes. I feel myself shrinking and burning up with guilt. I go straight to her desk and hand her the excuse slip. Just like all the other times, I say, "I was sick." I hate lying, but I have to. I don't want my parents to get in trouble.*

27   I finish my narrative about giving my phony excuses to my grade-school teachers and hand it in. I watch Mrs. Seth read it and, to my horror, she begins to cry. I know it must be because she is so disappointed, that what I have written is so far from what the assignment was meant to be that she doesn't know where to begin to correct it.

28   "Did you write this?" she asks me. Of course, she knows I wrote it, but she seems disbelieving. "You wrote this?" she asks again. Eventually I realize that she is not disappointed. Instead, she is telling me something incredible and wonderful. She is saying that my work is good, and that she is very happy with what I've given her. She is telling me that I can succeed here.

29   I have finished my first year of college with straight A's, and I will spend the summer picking crops in the fields. But in the fall, when my children return to school, so will I. I have a goal: to teach migrant children to speak English, to stand on their own two feet, to achieve their dreams. In helping them, I will be making my own dream come true.

With the help of her English teacher, Johanna Seth, Maria uses a word processor to edit one of her papers.

Vocabulary Check

1. In which sentence would the word **enraged** make sense?
   a. My mother was _____ to find out I had cleaned my room while she was out.
   b. The crowd was _____ when the little girl was finally saved from the burning building.
   c. The hiker was attacked by several _____ bees when he accidentally disturbed their hive.

2. In which sentence would the word **taunted** make sense?
   a. The boys _____ me because of my weight.
   b. The teacher _____ the class for doing so well on the history exam.
   c. Heavy snow _____ the school to cancel classes for two days.

3. In which sentence would the word **eligible** make sense?
   a. I was so _____ about going to the carnival today that I couldn't sleep last night.
   b. My brother could not read his own notes because his handwriting was too _____.
   c. The winner of the state spelling bee will be _____ to compete in the national contest.

Maria poses with her husband Alfonso after a day in the orange fields.

4. In the sentence below, the word **reprimand** means
   a. scold.
   b. ignore.
   c. praise.

   "I imagined returning to my mother, only to have her reprimand me, saying, 'What's the matter with you that you can't even stay married?'" (Paragraph 19)

5. In the sentence below, the word **resemblance** means
   a. difficulty.
   b. similarity.
   c. difference.

   "She works in the fields, as I did, but there is little resemblance between her life and mine." (Paragraph 25)

SCORE: (Number correct) _____ x 20 = _____ %

Reading Check

Central Point and Main Ideas

1. What is the central point of the reading?
   a. Maria's goal is to graduate from college and teach migrant children to achieve their dreams.
   b. With hard work and courage, Maria overcame a life of abuse to build a rich family life and aim for a degree in education.
   c. A book called *Dark Harvest*, which Maria read, is filled with inspiring stories about migrant workers.

2. What is the main idea of paragraph 7?
   a. Maria knew many children whose fathers had forgotten them.
   b. Maria's father started drinking heavily.
   c. Maria's father became more abusive as the years passed.

3. What is the main idea of paragraph 11?
   a. Maria had little control over what happened to her.
   b. Maria helped take care of the children whenever they got sick.
   c. Maria worked in the fields when the picking was good.

4. What is the main idea of paragraph 14?
   a. Mrs. Mercer, one of Maria's teachers, offered Maria a job at a Western clothing store.
   b. Mrs. Mercer, one of Maria's teachers, and her husband owned a Western clothing store.
   c. A job she got from a teacher made Maria begin to believe she could do more than field work.

Supporting Details

5. Maria enrolled in school under false names because
   a. her parents had criminal records and did not want to be identified.
   b. her parents were in the United States illegally.
   c. she enjoyed confusing her teachers about her name.

6. The first job that Maria got after meeting Mrs. Mercer was as a
   a. translator in the Western clothing store.
   b. cashier in the supermarket.
   c. teacher of migrant children.

7. After she read the book *Dark Harvest*, Maria
   a. abandoned her daughter and returned to Mexico.
   b. decided that she wanted to pick tomatoes for the rest of her life.
   c. was inspired to go to college and become a teacher.

Holding her younger daughter, Jasmine, Maria sits on her sofa at home with her older daughter, Antonietta, and her son, Korak.

Conclusions

8. You can conclude from paragraphs 1–3 that
   a. the teacher knows that Maria has been picking tomatoes instead of attending school.
   b. the teacher is worried about Maria being sick.
   c. Maria prefers working in the fields to attending school.

9. You can conclude from paragraph 12 that
   a. Maria felt guilty for not running away with her mother.
   b. Joel and Maria could not understand why their mother had left home.
   c. Maria's mother had prepared her children for the day she left her home.

10. You can conclude from paragraph 17 that
    a. Maria's "old-fashioned Mexican world" offered freedom and choice for women.
    b. Maria often wished to be part of the "old-fashioned Mexican world."
    c. The "old-fashioned Mexican world" was very strict about sex and marriage.

SCORE: (**Number correct**) _____ x 10 = _____%

Questions for Thinking and Discussion

1. Why do you think Mrs. Seth started to cry when she read Maria's narrative paragraph? Why do you think Maria believed that the teacher was disappointed with her paragraph?

2. Like her mother, Maria's daughter Antonietta works in the fields. In what ways is Antonietta's life different from Maria's life when Maria was a child?

3. What does Maria mean when she says she wants to teach migrant children to "stand on their own two feet"? Why do you think Maria feels so strongly that she wants to help children?

Ideas for Writing

1. Maria never let go of her dream of an education and a good job, even though she often received little support from the people around her. What dream do you hope to pursue? Write about your dream, explaining why it's important to you and why you won't let anyone change your mind.

2. Maria was scared about beginning classes at college, but she forced herself to do it anyway. Write a paper about a time when you were afraid of something new, but went ahead despite your fears. Describe the fears you had before beginning. Then tell whether the actual experience was similar to or different from what you had feared.

Jackie Leno Grant grew up in a comfortable world, surrounded by family and friends. Moving to another town changed all that. As a Native American in a nearly all-white school, Jackie felt out of place. Her unfair treatment at school could have made her bitter and rebellious. But Jackie refused to let bitterness rule her life.

11 / Jackie Leno Grant

Words to Watch

victimized (2): made a victim of
Thieves posing as carpenters have *victimized* elderly people in the neighborhood.

graveyard shift (10): work shift from about midnight to 8:00 a.m.
Since Dad got a *graveyard shift* job at the hospital, he sleeps all morning.

devastated (12): destroyed emotionally
Our neighbor was *devastated* when her best friend died.

assert (16): express with force
To be treated fairly, you must sometimes *assert* yourself.

ancient (19): very old
My favorite chair is an *ancient* rocker that my great-grandfather bought.

Jackie Leno Grant stands with her parents.

Jackie Leno Grant grew up listening to the stories her Native American grandfather told. There were sweet stories of his younger days, of fishing, of Jackie's father and his five brothers and sisters. But there were also other, more bitter tales. They were about how Jackie's great-grandparents and all their people were rounded up like cattle and taken from their homes in southern Oregon. Together with thousands of other Native Americans, they were driven hundreds of miles north, on foot and horseback, to the state's rocky western coast. Many of the elderly, the very young, and the sick died along the way. Those that survived were placed together with other Native Americans on a federal reservation. 1

It was there, on Oregon's western coast near Portland, that Jackie's grandparents lived and Jackie grew up. Despite their bitter past, Jackie's grandparents had a positive outlook. "They showed me that while you may be victimized°, you can refuse to take on the identity of a victim," says Jackie, now director of the Native American Program at Eastern Oregon State College. "I never learned bitterness toward people of other cultures, and I also never knew shame for being Indian. I always took pride in who I was." 2

That pride has carried Jackie through experiences that could easily have led to resentment, anger, and self-pity. 3

97

"When I was born, my mother, who is Norwegian-American, was very young, only 16," Jackie says. "She and my father, a Native American, had dated, and when she found she was pregnant, she didn't tell him. He didn't learn about me until after I was born. Then he came to find her and said, 'Come on. We'll get married, and I'll take you to my home.'" The three of them—Jackie, her father, and her mother—moved in with her father's parents.

Growing up in their house, Jackie developed a warm respect for her grandparents' way of life. "My grandparents thought a great deal of one another," she says. "The way they ran the household was very fair. For instance, my grandmother would take us to church on Sunday. Often my grandfather would choose not to go. She never said a word to try to change his mind. She just expected that he would have dinner started by the time we got home.

"The house was always open, always welcoming," she continues. "When people stopped by, it was assumed without any words that they would stay to eat with us."

Jackie's years in elementary school were happy ones. The students were primarily Native Americans, and although most of the teachers were white, the relations between the races were warm and accepting. But in the middle of sixth grade, Jackie's family moved forty-two miles to the town of Tillamook, Oregon. Job opportunities for her father, a logger, were better in that town. Although Tillamook had an Indian name, the Lenos were one of only two Native American families in town, and Jackie was the only Native American student in her class.

"The rest of sixth grade was good. My teacher, Mr. Peterson, seemed to care equally about all the kids in the class," Jackie remembers. "But that was my last happy year in school."

During seventh grade, Jackie became aware of racism around her. "It usually wasn't on the surface. But I became aware of people looking at me strangely, whispering about my family, expecting me to do something wrong," she says. "My parents were out of their element in Tillamook, too. They didn't make friends. There were no visitors in and out of the house."

Jackie's sense of loss was magnified when her beloved grandmother died. An important link to the loving, accepting world of her childhood was gone. At about the same time, Jackie's mother took a graveyard shift° job at a local mill. Jackie found herself getting less attention at home.

During the next couple of years at school, Jackie recalls, "I completely lost my bearings. School was a joke. My teachers didn't seem to care, and I cared less. I only went to the classes where I didn't feel humiliated, like choir and writing class."

Trying to connect with someone who might help, Jackie visited the guidance counselor and asked for information on trade schools. But the counselor stared at her and said, 'School isn't for you. You're just going to get married and have a bunch of kids.'" The counselor's words devastated° Jackie. "I'd been raised by people who had always told me, 'You can do whatever you want to do.' This was the first time I was told outright that I should not expect much out of life."

After that point, she says, "I hung out with my friends, smoked cigarettes, skipped school, and experimented with drugs."

Soon, matters got even worse. One day, Jackie and some friends went to the Dairy Queen for lunch and decided not to return to school. The next day they were called into the vice-principal's office. According to school policy, students caught skipping school for the first time were warned. The second time, they were suspended for three days. Jackie and her friends had never been caught before. The other kids in the group, who were all white, received the expected warning.

15   Jackie was told to leave school and never come back.

16   "I asked my mom to call the school and see why I wasn't treated like the other kids," says Jackie. "But she wouldn't. I know she was worried about my behavior, but I also think it was because she didn't feel she was part of that community. She didn't know how to assert° herself there." Instead, Jackie's mother took her to see a juvenile counselor, saying, "I don't know what my

daughter's doing. I can't control her." "So," Jackie says, "I was made a ward of the court and sent to a reform school, the Donald D. Long School for Girls in Portland."

17   At the school, Jackie was housed in a cottage with fifteen other girls. "I was searched. My luggage was searched. We were locked in our rooms at night. There were bars on the windows. Alarms sounded if someone left the campus. Newcomers weren't allowed visitors for a month because we were considered runaway risks during that time."

18   Despite the institutional feel of the place, Jackie learned to like the school, where she found the housemothers and teachers "nice and caring." "I did a lot of observing and thinking there," she says. "As I watched the other girls, I realized that I had more good things in my life than most of them had. I had a sense of myself and where I came from. Although we hadn't always gotten along, I had people who loved me and had tried their best to take care of me. It was obvious at mail-call time and visitors' day that many of the other girls had no one who cared at all."

19   Jackie began to think that she had arrived at the Donald D. Long School for a reason. A surprising visitor convinced her that she was right. "The housemother called to say someone wanted to see me," says Jackie. "I walked out to see an ancient° woman standing there. She said, 'You're Jacqueline Leno.' Then she looked at me for a long time and seemed so pleased. Finally, she stated, 'I knew your mother very well.' I was surprised. 'How do you know her?' I asked. She answered, 'This is the place where you were born.'"

20   Jackie's elderly visitor went on to explain that, years before, the school had been a home for unwed mothers. It was to this home that Jackie's mother had

gone as a confused, pregnant 15-year-old. The old woman, who had been an employee of the home, had taken a special interest in Jackie's young mother. "She spoke very fondly of my mom. Although she had retired years ago, she came back just to see me."

21 Learning that she had returned to the place of her birth filled Jackie with a sense of peace and purpose. "I knew I was completing a circle in my life, and I felt sure that things were falling into place for all the right reasons."

22 Jackie did well at the school, both academically and socially. After she had been there several months, a counselor called Jackie into her office. The counselor said, "Jackie, I just don't understand."

23 Jackie wondered if she had somehow managed to get into trouble. "What is it?" she asked.

24 "You study hard," the counselor said. "You don't lose your temper. You never get in fights. You don't run away. *Why* are you here?"

25 "I skipped school," Jackie answered.

26 Within days, the counselor and teachers had come up with a plan for Jackie. The school's principal and English teacher had recently gotten married. The couple, Curt and Karen Prickett, volunteered to be Jackie's foster parents. She moved into their home, but continued to attend classes at the school. During her senior year, the Pricketts helped Jackie land a half-time job at the immigration service office in Portland.

27 "I couldn't have asked for better parents," Jackie says. "We had a terrific relationship. They let me use their extra car to go home and see my parents on weekends. They helped me develop my social skills. They loved to give parties, and they would tell me my job at the party was to 'mingle.' I did a lot of growing up living with them."

28 After graduating from the Donald D. Long School, Jackie moved back to Tillamook and worked as a waitress. "It was a very happy time of my life," she recalls. "I found that a lot of people in Tillamook remembered me. Some knew me just as 'that girl who got railroaded out of town.' But others remembered me for more positive things. I saw that I had had more support in that town than I had realized. My own withdrawal had cut me off from people who would have helped me."

29 While working at the restaurant, Jackie met Steve Grant, a young man who was supporting himself as a carpenter as he worked his way through college. The two began dating. "Steve recognized in me abilities and drive that no one else had ever seen," Jackie says. "He became my mentor, encouraging me to try college classes."

30 Hesitantly, Jackie enrolled for a summer term at a community college. Her placement-test scores were "horrible" in most areas. "I needed every remedial class that college offered. But I wasn't at all discouraged by that," she explains. "As I looked at it, I hadn't failed. I simply hadn't prepared adequately for college work, and now I was doing something about that."

31 Jackie continued taking classes until the school's Native American counselor approached her one day. He had observed her love for learning and encouraged her to enroll in a four-year college. "You're not sure yet what you want to do with your life, and a four-year degree will offer you many more choices," he told her. Jackie decided to trust his advice, and she and Steve both enrolled at Eastern Oregon State College, in LaGrand.

32 At the end of her first year at Eastern, Steve graduated with his bachelor's degree. The two felt the time was

right to marry and begin a family, so Jackie left school. But eight years and three children later, Jackie decided to go back to college. She re-enrolled at Eastern Oregon and went to school for three solid years, including summers. She also held a part-time job in the school's Native American Program.

33   After she earned her degree in psychology in 1989, Jackie became director of Eastern Oregon's Native American program. In that position, she advises the school's Native American and Native Alaskan students, teaching them to reach out and get the help they need from the educational system. She, Steve, and their children—Neesha, Joaquin, and Jack— open their home to the students she advises, often hosting potluck dinners.

34   Jackie Grant's ancestors walked a "Trail of Tears." While Jackie's trail has had its own rough spots, her strong pride in her Native American heritage and the early lessons of her parents and grandparents have led her to achieve her personal goals. "They taught me that true satisfaction lies in doing your best, working your hardest, and reaching for the goals that you yourself have set, not those that anyone else has set for you," states Jackie. "I believed them when they told me that I could do whatever I wanted."

35   Now she is passing those lessons along to other young people.

Sharing a reading moment together are Jackie and her son Jack.

Vocabulary Check

1. In which sentence would the word **assert** make sense?
   a. My friend wants to be a science lab assistant, but he won't _____ himself enough to let the teacher know.
   b. To put this box together, you have to _____ tab *a* into slot *b*.
   c. People-watchers love to sit in the mall and _____ shoppers as they go about their business.

2. In which sentence would the word **ancient** make sense?
   a. If you have insulted him, you should do the _____ thing and apologize.
   b. I polished the kitchen floor until it was as _____ as glass.
   c. The museum's most valuable possession is the _____ mummy of an Egyptian king.

3. In the sentence below, the word **assumed** means
   a. disagreed.
   b. taken for granted.
   c. whispered.

   "'When people stopped by, it was assumed without any words that they would stay to eat with us.'" (Paragraph 6)

Jackie works with Tom Sanchez, one of the students she advises.

4. In the sentence below, the word **mentor** means
   a. enemy.
   b. advisor.
   c. boss.

   "'He became my mentor, encouraging me to try college classes.'" (Paragraph 29)

5. In the sentences below, the word **remedial** means
   a. intended to improve skills.
   b. advanced.
   c. free.

   "'I needed every remedial class that college offered. . . . I simply hadn't prepared adequately for college work, and now I was doing something about that.'" (Paragraph 30)

SCORE: **(Number correct)** _____ **x 20 =** _____%

Reading Check

Central Point and Main Ideas

1. What is the central point of the reading?
   a. School counselors must be trained to recognize their own racism.
   b. Jackie has overcome racism and other obstacles because of help from others and her belief in herself.
   c. Jackie's career in college was interrupted by the births of her children, but she managed to finish.

2. What is the main idea of paragraph 12?
   a. Jackie's visit to the school guidance counselor was discouraging instead of helpful.
   b. The guidance counselor thought that Jackie would have a lot of children someday.
   c. Jackie was interested in attending a trade school.

3. What is the main idea of paragraph 18?
   a. Many of Jackie's schoolmates did not receive letters or visits from their families.
   b. The teachers at the Donald D. Long School for Girls were nice and caring.
   c. Jackie realized she was better off than many of her schoolmates.

4. What is the main idea of paragraph 30?
   a. Jackie scored poorly on her college placement tests.
   b. Jackie didn't let her poor placement scores discourage her from starting college.
   c. Jackie decided to enroll at a local community college during the summer term.

Supporting Details

5. When Jackie's grandfather did not attend church, her grandmother
   a. criticized him to the children.
   b. did not speak to him for the rest of the day.
   c. expected him to start cooking the Sunday meal.

6. Jackie's adjustment to Tillamook was made more difficult by
   a. her father's losing his job.
   b. her grandmother's death.
   c. separation from her best friend.

7. What did the elderly woman who visited Jackie at the Donald D. Long reform school tell her?
   a. That the elderly woman was Jackie's real grandmother.
   b. That Jackie had been born at the school.
   c. That Jackie's parents had moved to another state.

Conclusions

8. You can conclude from paragraph 5 that
   a. Jackie's grandmother never did any of the cooking for the family.
   b. Jackie learned a lot about getting along with others from observing her grandparents.
   c. Jackie's grandfather did not want his wife, children, or grandchildren to go to church on Sundays.

9. You can conclude from paragraphs 22–26 that
   a. Jackie's behavior grew worse after she moved into a foster home.
   b. the Pricketts had never met Jackie before becoming her foster parents.
   c. Jackie's teachers thought she did not belong in a reform school.

10. You can conclude from paragraph 28 that
    a. as a teenager, Jackie might have gotten along better in Tillamook if she had been more open and friendly.
    b. the people who remembered Jackie for positive reasons were all Native Americans.
    c. Jackie was embarrassed to be seen in Tillamook again.

SCORE: (Number correct) _____ x 10 = _____%

*Posing with Jackie are her husband, Steve, and their children
(left to right), Jack, Neesha, and Joaquin.*

With her son, Jackie visits the gravesites of her Native American grandparents.

Questions for Thinking and Discussion

1. How was Jackie's behavior affected by what she was told by the guidance counselor at the school in Tillamook?

2. What valuable lessons do you think Jackie learned as a result of her time at the Donald D. Long reform school?

3. Indirectly, Jackie's grandparents taught her a good deal about getting along with others. Think of an adult in your life whose behavior you admire. What have you learned from that person about how to treat others?

Ideas for Writing

1. When Jackie learned that the Donald D. Long School was the place of her birth, she felt a "sense of peace" and believed that everything in her life was "falling into place." Write a paper describing a time when you, too, felt happy and hopeful about the future.

2. When Jackie and her friends were caught skipping school, Jackie was expelled while the other kids were only warned. Have you, or has someone you know, ever been singled out for punishment that you thought was unfair? Write a paper explaining what happened and how you felt about it.

12 / Kala White

Words to Watch

contenders (4): people in a competition
Both boxers were *contenders* for the heavy-weight crown.

ego (6): sense of self-importance
That student has a big *ego*—he thinks he's the smartest, most talented person he knows.

optimism (11): a tendency to expect good things to happen
The woman cast her line into the water with great *optimism*, sure that she would soon catch a fish.

elapsed (21): passed (said of time)
When I woke up from my nap, I was surprised to find that three hours had *elapsed*.

intimidating (23): scary; threatening
After getting some tutoring, I no longer find math class so *intimidating*.

Kala White reads on his bed at home.

Chumps who talk junk, then fake, front, and stall 1
Can't amount to half the styles I throw away,
Goin' down in history as the best in my day
Cuz only fresh rhymes I'm making, all records I be breakin',
from shock heads be shakin', I'm simply breath-takin'!

I was a freshman at Cass Tech, a 2 very challenging high school in Detroit. If you weren't ready to accept its challenge from day one, you were buried under an academic avalanche. I wasn't ready. When I arrived at Cass, all I was worried about was becoming popular as a good rapper. School work came second. Sometimes it never came at all.

I was in a rap group called the Young 3 MCz. Our favorite pastime was sitting in the back of the classroom, making fun of the students who were trying to learn. "Listen to that fool," we would say, laughing loudly. Sometimes we would cough to disturb a student reading to the class. It was kind of fun. Unfortunately, I had to pay for all that fun. I was kicked out at the end of the year, and I didn't find that amusing at all.

Shooting out of Cass Tech like a 4 meteor, I crash-landed in Northern High. As my sophomore year progressed, I became a much better rapper. I was one of the students who went to school only to compete in rapping. My brother Kojo was right there with me. He was like Don King; I was like Mike Tyson. He would set them up, and I would take them out. "Hey, Kala, we got another challenge," he would say, speed-walking to the lavatory. The lavatories were the rappers' battle grounds in this school. There were always lyric wars being fought, and I was one of the top contenders°. I never lost!

5   *Mo' funky than socks I got you smelling a rhythm*
       When I gives 'em what I got I hits 'em with my hypnotism
       Under my spell I gets 'em hooked like fish
       Any rapper try to diss he'll end up my main dish.

6   My ego° ballooned. I felt as though I was on top of the world. In reality, I was digging myself into an ever-deeper hole. I attended class less and less often. Days stretched into weeks, and weeks grew to months. Once again I was kicked out of school, but this time it was only a little past mid-semester. I had to wait until the next year to enroll in a new school.

7   Fall fell upon me. It was time to give this school thing another try. As I walked through the graffiti-filled halls of Northwestern High, my third school in three years, I knew I didn't want to be there. At Cass Tech, all I had to worry about was schoolwork. At Northwestern, the list of things to be concerned about ran much longer. Schoolwork was still a major problem. I hadn't gone to school seriously since the eighth grade. The gangs, the fights, the gunshots, and the occasional news of somebody's death eventually became overwhelming.

8   I remember my defeated, hopeless feeling on the day I decided to quit school. It was fourth hour, my English class. I guess it had been a week, maybe two, since I had made an appearance there. Twenty minutes into the class period, as I sat there not paying any attention, it happened.

9   "Kala, would you like to tell us the answer?"

10   For the first time I could remember in that class, everyone's eyes were locked on me, and I hadn't even heard the question. I stalled for a few seconds, breaking into a cold sweat, before responding, "I don't know." Some of the students chuckled while others just smirked. Embarrassment doesn't begin to explain what I felt. I walked out of the school after that class, threw my barely used notebook in a trash can, and never returned.

11   When I walked through the front door of my home, I knew I had a long evening ahead of me. My father was aware of how I was doing in school, but he wasn't ready to accept my failure. I went upstairs to his room, knocked on the door, humbly entered, and began to plead my case. "Daddy, I was thinking . . . " I began, then blurted, "I'm going to drop out of school." He looked at me, blank-faced, and then asked, "So, you're giving up?" I stood speechless. Until that moment, I hadn't looked at it as giving up. I thought of it as a necessary step toward getting my life together. Dropping out of school would break the cycle of failure, I told myself. One look at my father's face told me that he did not share my optimism°. "Well, if you want to be a quitter, that's up to you," he said in disgusted tones, "but if you plan on being one here, you're going to have to get and keep a job."

12   I worked at McDonald's for all of three weeks before I got fired. After that I spent my time either doing nothing or hanging around the wrong people, doing the wrong things, developing a bad attitude. My attitude towards my father changed, too. I said disrespectful things in inappropriate tones. Even then, he

didn't kick me out of the house. He knew putting me out at that time would have been my death sentence. I was on the edge, bordering on a life of crime. Hanging in the streets with my cousins, brothers, and our boys, I began believing no one in this world was tougher than I was. I no longer listened when the conversation rose above the street level of life. I spent my time in rooms where the talk was about robbing people, robbing banks, and selling drugs. I, a rookie at this new life, was trying to learn all the rules of the street before I crossed over.

13   One night as I walked out of the house after midnight, my father confronted me. "Where are you going?" he asked. I shot back, "I'm going out!" My father was finally sick of my attitude and said what was on his mind. "All right, you don't want to listen to anything I've been telling you to do," he said. "But you will

one day—if you live long enough." I walked out, slamming the door behind me.

14   When I reached my destination, I was greeted with a Colt .45 forty-ounce beer. I rhythmically strolled through the smoke-filled room, rocking my head to the rap booming from the radio. I found a seat and began to drink. As the icy, bitter liquid spilled down my throat, altering my mind, I thought about my father's words. My eyes drifted around the room, filled with high and drunk young black men like me. "This is how I want to live," I thought to myself. I made a drunken decision to spend the rest of my years living the street life to the fullest.

15   I lived up to that decision until one fateful night. I was cruising through the southwest side of Detroit with my older cousin Tony and my younger brother Paul. Tony and Paul had been drinking. I had gotten sloppy drunk the night before, so I told them I would just chill out. It was about two o'clock in the morning when we pulled up to a red light at the corner of Warren and Livernois, next to the White Castle restaurant that stood on the corner. In front of the White Castle were two pay phones. A group of seven or eight guys were standing by the phones. When we pulled up to the light, a staring contest began. They were looking for trouble, and we, being young and stupid enough to play the street game, didn't avoid it.

16   "Who they looking at?" we began asking one another. They were trying to front us off. It wouldn't have been "gangster" of us not to stare back. Instead of keeping straight on Warren, we turned onto Livernois, driving right past them. Our eyes were fastened to theirs. They were on the right side of the car, the passenger side, my side. As we drove closer to them, the tension increased. Right before we became parallel to them, one of

them made a quick move. His hand emerged from his jacket. I saw a flash of silver, and then I quickly ducked down. One . . . two . . . three gunshots rang out, slicing through the silence of the night. I didn't feel anything hit me. The car jerked forward, then began slowing. My brother's voice stammered out, "Kala . . . Kala! Tony got shot."

17   I looked over at Tony without raising my head. I will never forget what I saw. Tony was shot in the head. His hand was slipping from the steering wheel as his head slowly fell against the neck support of his seat. I sat motionless, shocked, for several seconds. I was aware of Paul, trapped in the back seat of Tony's small two-door Ford Escort. As I raised my head, I caught a glimpse of my passenger-side mirror. It reflected seven or eight guys running up behind the car.

18   The car was coasting towards the curb, so I tried to gain control of it. I grabbed the wheel and turned it away from the curb, but Tony's thick leg blocked the gas pedal. I turned for a quick look behind us. They were about fifteen feet away. With all the strength I had, I pushed Tony's leg out of the way and stamped on the gas pedal. From the passenger seat, running red lights along the way, I sped all the way down Livernois until we reached the gas station on Michigan Avenue. About one minute after we pulled into the station, the police arrived.

19   As we sat in the back seat of the squad car, my eyes were locked on Tony. I couldn't believe what had just happened—one second we were talking, and the next Tony was dead. The horror of that night made me realize that I had chosen the wrong path in life by trying to be a gangster.

20   Trying to correct my life, which had so badly fallen off course, I found a job working at a mailing company in Livonia.

The pay was low, and the work was hard. I was making five dollars per hour, working ten hours a day. The only thing that kept me going was the hope of being able to get my own studio equipment so I could make music for my raps. I tried saving, but car expenses alone ate up my checks. I knew I had to do something, and one day when my boss barked one command too many at me, I did. I told him that I quit, but not in those exact words.

Sitting on a front porch in his neighborhood, Kala chats with his cousin.

21   For a few weeks I sat at home and thought about my options. Almost two years had elapsed° since I quit school. During that time all I had accomplished was working a few odd jobs, keeping myself alive, and keeping my car half running. For some time, my mother had been telling me to study and get my high-school general equivalency diploma (GED) so I could go to college. I never really listened, until one night she said something that really made me think. "Kala, all you have to do is look at the year that has just passed, and you'll see your future." I just sat there with my usual "Will you hurry up and end this lecture" look on my face. However, this time I heard everything she said. I was alarmed by the thought of a lifetime of years like the last one. The next day, I went out and purchased a GED

preparatory book with the last few dollars I had.

22   I studied through depressing early mornings, frustrating afternoons, and exhausting late nights. It sometimes took a whole day just to figure out one problem or answer one question, but I got it done. The most shocking thing of all was that writing my own essays actually became fun—much like writing my raps, which I no longer found the time to do. It was the beginning of winter when I began studying. The coming of the summer melted away the ice and snow from the Detroit streets. At the same time, my scholastic rebirth thawed my brain, iced up from a long mental deep freeze. I called the GED testing center, set up my appointment to take the test, and continued to study.

23   When the big day came, I felt ready. The GED test was at 8:00 a.m. I arrived at 7:30. I drove into the weed-infested cement and gravel lot, parked, and then sat in my car for a while. The huge old building stood before me, inviting yet intimidating°. Sitting there in something like a hypnotic trance, I repeatedly said out loud, "I am not going to fail this test." My confidence peaked, yanked me from the car, and marched me in as a man on a mission. I didn't come down from that mental high until the next day as I sat in the hallway with the others, awaiting our results. Finally I heard, "White, Kala White, you're next."

24   The instructor opened up the enve-lope and looked over my score sheet. Then he looked up at me, stuck out his hand and said, "Congratulations." I wildly shook his hand, sloppily signed a few dotted lines, and darted out the building. Slamming my car door behind me, I burned rubber out of the parking lot. I raced across town to my house and told everyone what I had achieved! It had been a long time since I felt I had accomplished anything. Then I waited impatiently for the coming fall and the start of college.

25   Now, with my first semester of school at Henry Ford Community College behind me, I know that more accomplishments lie ahead. I'm going to major in English. Throughout all those years of rapping, I developed a love for writing. Now I earn straight A's in my writing classes. Every day when I return home from school, I feel as if I've done something worthwhile.

26   When I think back on all those years of throwing away my time and energy, I don't feel embarrassed or ashamed, surprisingly. All the things I've gone through have strengthened me. Those past experiences, good and bad, are the foundation of my present character. My philosophy of life is to live with constant consideration for tomorrow. If I stumble here and there in my academic journey, I will use that moment of weakness as a learning experience. I know that as long as I keep things planned and in perspective, I can hurdle any obstacle that stands in my path.

Vocabulary Check

1. In which sentence would the word **optimism** make sense?
   a. My uncle can't drive after dark because of his _____.
   b. Grandmother's _____ helps her start every day in a good mood.
   c. The _____ between the two close friends led to a noisy argument.

2. In which sentence would the word **elapsed** make sense?
   a. When the temperature rose to ninety-eight, an elderly man _____ on the sidewalk.
   b. When the man _____ to give his speech to the class, his hands began to shake.
   c. Two years have _____ since I last saw my cousin.

3. In the sentence below, the word **avalanche** means
   a. reward for hard work.
   b. large amount of material.
   c. visit.

   "If you weren't ready to accept its challenge from day one, you were buried under an academic avalanche." (Paragraph 2)

4. In the sentences below, the word **blurted** means
   a. questioned.
   b. demanded angrily.
   c. said suddenly.

   "I went upstairs to his room, knocked on the door, humbly entered, and began to plead my case. 'Daddy, I was thinking . . .' I began, then blurted, 'I'm going to drop out of school.'" (Paragraph 11)

Kala reads in the library at Henry Ford Community College.

5. In the sentences below, the word **confronted** means
   a. avoided.
   b. warmly supported.
   c. faced in a challenging way.

   "One night as I walked out of the house after midnight, my father confronted me. 'Where are you going?' he asked. . . . My father was finally sick of my attitude and said what was on his mind." (Paragraph 13)

SCORE: (Number correct) _____ x 20 = _____%

Reading Check

Central Point and Main Ideas

1. What is the central point of the reading?
   a. Rapping got in the way of Kala's education.
   b. By getting into a staring contest, Kala put his life at risk.
   c. A shocking event and parental support turned Kala away from a gangster lifestyle.

2. What is the main point of paragraph 7?
   a. When Kala was at Northwestern High School, his life continued to go downward.
   b. Kala began to hear occasional news of somebody's death.
   c. When fall came, Kala entered Northwestern High School.

3. What is the main point of paragraph 10?
   a. Kala did not hear what the teacher asked him.
   b. An embarrassing classroom incident caused Kala to quit school.
   c. The whole class looked at Kala when the teacher asked him a question.

4. What is the main point of paragraph 19?
   a. Kala's eyes locked on Tony.
   b. Tony was alive and talking one minute, and the next he was dead.
   c. Tony's sudden death made Kala realize he had chosen a bad lifestyle.

Supporting Details

5. At Northern High, the rap competitions were held in the
   a. gymnasium.
   b. parking lot.
   c. lavatory.

6. Tony was Kala's
   a. friend.
   b. brother.
   c. cousin.

7. Kala decided to study for a general equivalency diploma (GED) because
   a. he preferred studying to working.
   b. he did not want the life he had lived the previous two years.
   c. studying would give him more time to work on his rapping.

Conclusions

8. You can conclude from paragraph 18 that
   a. if Kala had not taken control of the car, he and Paul might have been shot.
   b. the men running after the car wanted to help Tony.
   c. the car was almost out of gas.

9. You can conclude from paragraph 21 that
    a. Kala's mother did not understand her son very well.
    b. Kala had found the last year of his life depressing.
    c. Kala was not interested in going to college.

10. You can conclude from paragraph 26 that
    a. Kala wishes he could live his life over again.
    b. Kala is not convinced that college is for him.
    c. Kala intends to continue to learn from his mistakes.

SCORE: **(Number correct)** _____ **x 10 =** _____ **%**

Questions for Thinking and Discussion

1. What do you think draws young people like Kala into the street life and "gangster" culture?

2. Explain what Kala means in paragraph 12 by each of the following:

    "He knew putting me out at that time would have been my death sentence."

    "I, a rookie at this new life, was trying to learn all the rules of the street before I crossed over."

3. Have you, like Kala, ever seen something bad happen to someone else and thought, "That could have been me"? Describe the experience.

Kala studies in his room at home.

Sitting with Kala are his parents, Bennie and Paulette White.

Ideas for Writing

1. Kala's parents did not give up on him. Think of someone whom you can rely on for support and encouragement. Write a paper about a specific time that person was there for you when you needed help.

2. All of us have made mistakes that we can learn from. Think about something you did or said that you later regretted. In a paper, describe what happened, and explain what the incident taught you.

A new country, a new language, new customs, and that awful macaroni and cheese! How could a girl from Beijing, China, adjust to life in an Iowa country town? Read Xinrong "Cindy" Liu's story and find out.

13 / Xinrong "Cindy" Liu

Words to Watch

rural (2): of the country
Do you know the children's story about a *rural* mouse who visits his cousin in the city?

destination (6): the place one is going
Before our trip to the Grand Canyon, we learned everything that we could about our *destination*.

startling (7): surprising; shocking
It was *startling* to hear a sudden knock at the door at midnight.

inquisitive (8): curious
At first our new kitten was shy, but then she became *inquisitive* and began to explore her new home.

adapted (29): adjusted
The girls felt homesick until they *adapted* to life at summer camp.

Cindy Liu reviews notes in a student union lounge.

Beijing is the capital of the People's Republic of China. Its eleven million residents make it one of the world's most crowded cities. High-rise apartment buildings sit jammed together. Open-air farmers' markets hum with activity. Streams of people rush along the sidewalks throughout the day and far into the night. 1

Shenandoah is a rural° town in the southwest corner of Iowa. Six thousand people live there. Large homes sit along the quiet, tree-lined streets. Huge tracts of farmland lie along the outskirts of town. It's the kind of town where people greet each other by name as they pass on the sidewalk. 2

The Chinese city and the American town are about thirteen thousand miles apart. In culture, customs, and language, the two places are even more separated. Xinrong "Cindy" Liu has had to struggle to cross the great distance between these two worlds. 3

Cindy Liu's long journey began in the late 1980's, when her father visited the United States. During a stop in Shenandoah, Iowa, he stayed with an American family, the Perrys. Years before, the Perrys had hosted foreign exchange students from China. When they heard that Mr. Liu's daughter, Xinrong, was a high-school student, they asked if she might want to spend her senior high-school year in the United States. 4

5   Mr. Liu returned to China and told Xinrong about the Perrys' suggestion. "I said 'Sure, wow, what a great opportunity,'" she remembers. Although the idea of leaving her family so far behind was scary, her chief reaction was one of enthusiasm. "I'd always been adventurous. I've always liked trying new things," she says. "When I was younger, I moved a lot and spent time living with my grandparents. I guess growing up that way helped make me very open to change."

6   Xinrong—who later adopted the American name Cindy—left Beijing in September, 1990. On the long flight from China to San Francisco, she sat with a friend of her father's. But when they arrived at the San Francisco airport, Cindy was on her own. She boarded a plane for her destination°, Kansas City.

7   The flight to Kansas City was Cindy's first real taste of life in a foreign land. "I had mixed feelings," she remembers. "Everyone around me was talking, and I couldn't understand a word. The signs were all in English. The people looked so strange." After a lifetime of living among Chinese people, the sudden mix of white, black, and brown-skinned people, with just an occasional Asian face, was startling°.

8   But even in those first somewhat confusing hours of dealing with her new environment, Cindy's inquisitive° spirit came through.

9   "I don't know why I wasn't more frightened," she says today. "I look back at it and think, 'There you were, barely 18 years old and all alone in this new world—you *should* have been scared.' But I was more curious than anything else. I understood only about 10 percent of what people said to me, and when I talked, it was v-e-e-r-r-y s-lo-o-wly. But everyone tried hard to communicate with me."

10   The Perry family met Cindy at the Kansas City International Airport and drove her to her new home in Shenandoah. Here another shock awaited.

11   "We pulled into the driveway of this huge house, sitting all by itself up on a hill," Cindy says. "It had a huge backyard. I was just astonished that this house held only four people, the Perrys and their two sons. I didn't know what to say."

12   The size of American houses and the amount of open space still surprises Cindy. In her home city of Beijing, she explains, a family of four lives in a small two-bedroom apartment in a high-rise building. The city streets are filled constantly with a stream of walking and bicycling people. Stores are open until 2:00 or 3:00 a.m., and even at that hour, they are filled with shoppers. By contrast, Cindy was astonished when she and the Perrys would shop in Shenandoah's supermarket and be the only people in an aisle. "I'd think to myself, 'Is the store really open? Maybe we're not supposed to be here!'" Cindy remembers.

13   Soon after arriving in Iowa, Cindy enrolled for her senior year at the local high school. The adjustment was difficult.

14   "I had studied English at school, but it was textbook English," she says. "We didn't practice conversation very much, and when we did it was basic stuff like 'Hello. How are you?' or 'It is a nice day today.' I arrived in America knowing perhaps five hundred to seven hundred English words. And when I was suddenly in the middle of an English-speaking school, I think I forgot every one of them.

15   "I didn't understand my teachers at all," Cindy continues. "In American History class, the teacher would put slides covered with writing up on the screen. They were facts about the Civil War, information that was common knowledge to the other students, but I

didn't understand them. So I'd begin madly scribbling the words down, but before I got half-done the teacher would put up a new slide."

16   Daily experiences like that left Cindy feeling inadequate and depressed. She felt herself dropping behind her classmates, an unusual experience for her. "I am a competitive person, and in China I was always a good student," she says. "Things came easily to me. So it was very, very hard for me to sit there and know people saw me as someone who couldn't keep up."

17   One of Cindy's most frustrating experiences occurred when she took a supposedly easy class. "I signed up for home economics, which is supposed to be a snap," she says. "It was *terrible* for me." When the mid-term exam came around, Cindy was determined to do her best. It wasn't easy. "The test was full of super-market brand names and questions about using credit cards—all stuff that didn't mean anything to me." One question in particular puzzled Cindy. It started out, "You have two loads of laundry, one navy and one white . . . " Cindy looked up the word *navy* in her dictionary and got even more confused. "I asked myself, 'What does laundry have to do with warships?'"

18   At the end of ninety minutes, when Cindy was still working, the teacher offered to let her take the test home. Frustrated and embarrassed, Cindy felt singled out yet again. "I know she meant to be kind, but I felt as if she were saying, 'Oh, I understand. You're not capable.' I really hated knowing that people viewed me that way."

19   Adjusting to the American tendency to show emotions openly was hard for Cindy as well. "Chinese people are taught to be calm and reserved," she explains. "You're not expected to laugh if you're happy, or frown if you're sad. If you do those things, your parents scold you and say, 'No one wants to be bothered with your emotions. Deal with them privately!'" Not only did Americans show their emotions, but they often did it loudly. "In China," Cindy continues, "if you ever heard someone screaming, you would know either that there was something terribly wrong or that the person was crazy." Given that background, Cindy was amazed when she attended her first American football game. "I was shocked to see people of all ages—even respected elders—jumping out of their seats and screaming. I didn't even know how to scream!"

20   Cindy's head and heart were full of impressions of her new home. Some were positive. Others were negative. Many were confusing. But she found most of them impossible to express.

21   "The American students were nice, but I certainly wasn't one of the gang," she says. "It took a lot of patience at the

beginning to try to talk with me, and teenagers generally are not really patient people. I slowly got better at English and could talk more about objects and facts, but it was a long time before I could describe how I was *feeling*. I couldn't argue or persuade or do anything with language that would really let other people know who I was inside."

22   The houses, the culture, the language, the classes—and then there was the food. During her first months in the United States, Cindy lost weight trying to adjust to the American diet.

23   "In China, we eat mostly rice and vegetables and very little red meat," she explains. "There were some things I liked right away, like pizza and spaghetti, but other things were very strange to me. Like big hunks of meat. And salad! In China, you stir-fry vegetables. You don't eat a big bowl of them raw. And macaroni and cheese!" Cindy shakes her head in disbelief. "The Perry boys *loved* it. That was something I never got used to!"

24   Cindy missed her favorite Chinese dishes, like *chun juan*, crisp spring rolls made to celebrate the Chinese New Year, and *jiao zi*, boiled dumplings stuffed with vegetables, meat, or seafood. She visited Chinese restaurants in the Shenandoah area but was generally disappointed. "I'd taste things and say, 'Well, interesting, but not like Mom's!'" she laughs.

25   Although Cindy can smile now when she remembers her first months in the United States, the experience was not funny at the time. "Emotionally, it was very difficult," she explains. "I cried in bed at night many times, wanting to just give up."

26   Not ready to give up, Cindy pushed herself to seek the help she needed. "I learned to ask and ask and ask some more," she says. To ask for special help in itself was a big adjustment for a Chinese student. "In China, we are taught from the beginning never to question authority. No one would ever interrupt a teacher with a question. It wasn't easy for me to believe that I could stop a teacher and say, 'What do you mean by . . . ' But I learned. And I realized that people are generally more than willing to help—*if you ask them*. The drive to learn had to come from inside me. I couldn't sit and wait for people to offer help."

Surrounded by her bear collection, Cindy sits in her bedroom.

27   Cindy's English is close to perfect now and almost accent-free. People often express surprise at how well she speaks. "They say to me, 'I know people who have been in this country twenty years and can't speak English yet!' But I think that is because they've stayed in their own circles. They've not forced themselves to interact with Americans. I didn't have that opportunity—there were practically no other Chinese people where I was. If there had been more, I probably would

have spent my time with them and not learned as much. But now, I'm glad it happened the way it did."

28   By the time Cindy graduated from high school, she had decided to remain in the United States. "I found myself fitting into the environment and really liking it, so I began looking into colleges." She enrolled at Iowa Western Community College. While there, she worked as a tutor and presented programs about China to civic clubs and church organizations.

29   Now she is a student at Kansas State University (KSU), where she will graduate this year with a degree in computer science. At KSU, she found a large population of other Chinese students, but she does not spend much time with them. "Earlier, I needed the support of people from my own country," she says. "But now, I've adapted° to the American way of life, and most of my friends are Americans. Also, most of the Chinese at KSU are graduate students, older than I am, with their own families, so I don't have so much in common with them."

30   Cindy's matter-of-fact attitude makes her success in this country sound easily gained. But her determination has carried her over obstacles that would have discouraged many people.

31   She barely mentions her financial struggles, yet there have been many of them. She works constantly to earn money for her college tuition and spends countless hours researching and applying for scholarships. One summer she worked almost around the clock at three different jobs. During the day, she made machine parts on a factory assembly line. In the evening, she worked as a waitress. She spent the nights as a companion to an elderly woman who had suffered a stroke.

32   But she does not think much about the negative. "I have never been in a situation that I felt helpless to improve. I truly believe the saying, 'When God closes a door, He opens a window.'" Cindy feels the secret to success is to look for that window and use all one's powers to climb through it.

33   At Cindy's high-school graduation, a counselor gave her a card. On it was this verse:

Only as high as I reach can I grow;
Only as deep as I look can I see;
Only as much as I dream can I be.

34   In Beijing and the American Midwest, Cindy Liu has reached, looked, and dreamed. Who knows where her curiosity and belief in herself will take her next?

Vocabulary Check

1. In which sentence would the word **adapted** make sense?
   a. My brother _____ to get up early today, but his alarm clock didn't ring.
   b. The gentle German shepherd _____ the motherless kitten and kept it safe.
   c. When I first moved to Minnesota I was always cold, but now I've _____ to the weather.

2. In which sentence would the word **startling** make sense?
   a. I like some serious movies, but my favorites are _____ comedies.
   b. It was _____ to see how different our neighbor looked after her heart attack.
   c. Children like my grandfather because he has a calm, gentle manner and a _____ voice.

3. In the sentence below, the word **astonished** means
   a. angry.
   b. relieved.
   c. surprised.

   " 'I was just astonished that this house held only four people, the Perrys and their two sons.' " (Paragraph 11)

While going to school, Cindy lives with her "honorary parents," Sherry Wright and Dennis Blair.

4. In the sentence below, the word **frustrating** means
   a. discouraging.
   b. organized.
   c. friendly.

   "One of Cindy's most frustrating experiences occurred when she took a supposedly easy class." (Paragraph 17)

5. In the sentence below, the word **reserved** means
   a. showing little feeling.
   b. bad-tempered.
   c. enthusiastic.

   " 'Chinese people are taught to be calm and reserved,' she explains. 'You're not expected to laugh if you're happy. . . .' " (Paragraph 19)

SCORE: **(Number correct)** _____ x 20 = _____%

Reading Check

Central Point and Main Ideas

1. What is the central point of the reading?
   a. Teachers shouldn't embarrass foreign students by giving them special treatment.
   b. Cindy learned that the food and housing in the United States are very different from those in China.
   c. To succeed in the United States, Cindy has overcome loneliness and adjusted to differences in language and culture.

2. What is the main idea of paragraph 5?
   a. Cindy had spent part of her childhood living with her grandparents.
   b. Cindy felt some fear at the idea of leaving her family behind in China.
   c. Since Cindy always enjoyed adventure and change, she liked the idea of going to the United States.

3. What is the main idea of paragraph 19?
   a. Chinese people are expected not to laugh even if they are happy.
   b. It wasn't easy for Cindy to adjust to the open, sometimes loud way that Americans express themselves.
   c. At American football games, people of all ages express their emotions very loudly.

4. What is the main idea of paragraph 26?
   a. Cindy's experience in the United States got easier once she began asking for the help she needed.
   b. Chinese teachers are not used to being questioned by their students.
   c. Cindy had to make a lot of adjustments as she became used to United States schools.

Supporting Details

5. In coming to the United States, Cindy went from
   a. a city with many races to a country with many races.
   b. a big, crowded city to a small country town.
   c. her parents' home to the home of American relatives.

6. The thing that surprised Cindy most about the Perrys' house was
   a. its furniture.
   b. its color.
   c. its size.

7. In China, Cindy had been
   a. unusually shy.
   b. a competitive student.
   c. very talkative.

8. Attending a football game, Cindy was surprised by
   a. the violence of the game.
   b. the screaming of the fans.
   c. the use of so much open space for a football field.

Conclusions

9. You can conclude from paragraphs 17 and 18 that
   a. Cindy had never done her own laundry.
   b. the home economics class taught students how to do laundry on a warship.
   c. it was embarrassing for Cindy to do poorly in a class that was supposed to be easy.

10. You can conclude from paragraph 27 that
    a. if Cindy had met people from China when she was in Shenandoah, she would not have worked as hard to learn English.
    b. Cindy knows many Americans who visited China and did not learn Chinese very well.
    c. when she first arrived in the United States, Cindy was glad that there were very few other Chinese people in Shenandoah.

SCORE: **(Number correct)** _____ **x 10 =** _____ %

Cindy works at her part-time job at the computer resource center on campus.

Meeting with Cindy is her computer science professor, David Gustafson.

Questions for Thinking and Discussion

1. How does life in the Chinese city of Beijing differ from life in your town? What adjustment problems do you think you would have if you lived in Beijing for a year?

2. Cindy felt out of place in her American high school because so much was new to her. Think of a place or situation where you did not seem to fit in. What made you feel out of place? What did you do to make yourself feel more comfortable?

3. Cindy said that when she first came to the United States, "American students were nice, but I certainly wasn't one of the gang." What do you think the American students could have done to make Cindy's adjustment easier? Have you ever gone to school with a student who didn't speak much English? How did you and the other students react to that person?

Ideas for Writing

1. Cindy is described as adventurous, competitive, and hard-working. In a paper titled "My Image of Myself," write about two or three qualities that describe you, and provide examples of each quality.

2. Cindy jumped at the opportunity to come to the United States. What opportunity would you jump at? Describe in detail the place you would like to go, the person you would like to meet, or the thing you would like to do. In addition, explain why that place, person, or thing so appeals to you.

Growing up in a tough section of Santa Monica, Oscar de la Torre learned that poor Mexican-American kids like him were "supposed" to be gang members and criminals. But something inside him made him look at the wasted lives around him and say, "Not me." In his struggle to succeed, he has provided a role model for kids coming up after him.

14 / Oscar de la Torre

Words to Watch

lethal (6): capable of causing death
The man was arrested for carrying a *lethal* weapon into the school.

diversity (18): variety
I like a *diversity* of friends—not only friends who are just like me.

exhilarating (20): producing happy excitement; thrilling
After two weeks of rain, it is *exhilarating* to feel the sun on my face.

assured (20): made to feel sure about something
We felt relief when the math teacher *assured* us we could retake the exam.

excel (23): do better than others
The boys *excel* at math, and they are also excellent in music.

Oscar de la Torre speaks at a community meeting.

Oscar de la Torre does not own a car. He lives in a small apartment in a building infested with cockroaches. He is thousands of dollars in debt for his education. Yet Oscar holds on to something more valuable than anything he could ever buy: a dream to help his people. This dream has earned him a high-school diploma, a college degree, and acceptance into graduate school at the University of Texas.

The seventh of eight children, Oscar grew up in Santa Monica, California, in a ten-block stretch of crime and poverty called Pico Corridor. His parents were hard workers, but they were unable to speak English and were unfamiliar with American culture. As a result, they were not able to prepare their children for the dangers of the Corridor.

As a Mexican-American, Oscar was taught many lessons on the streets of Santa Monica. He remembers when, at the age of 8, he had his first experience with a police officer. "I got a ticket for riding on the handlebars of someone's bike," he explains. "When the officer gave me the piece of paper, he told me that I would grow up to be another Mexican criminal. I was so young, I didn't know any better, so I believed him." This lesson was further taught by the world around him. "I saw white folks with nice houses and nice cars. Since everything white was good, I just thought everything brown was bad, and since I was brown, I had to be bad too."

4 By the time he was 10, Oscar had become what he thought he was supposed to be: a criminal.

5 First, he began hanging out with teenagers in the neighborhood. "I looked up to the older kids," he says. "I wanted them to like me, and since they had money, I wanted to be like them." The means to much of that money was stealing. When he was nine years old, Oscar and his friends started stealing bicycles. Later, they moved up to wallets and then car stereos. "It just kept getting worse and worse. We were stealing bigger and more expensive things." Once, he was caught stealing and spent an evening in jail.

6 However, theft wasn't the only destructive force in Oscar's life. In the mid-1980s, lethal° drugs began to spread through the Corridor. At 11 years old, Oscar watched as two of his friends took their first hits of crack cocaine. "My one friend's heart was beating so hard I could see it pounding through his T-shirt. Watching him, I knew crack wasn't good." Oscar was so scared he refused to try the drug, but his two friends are still addicts today.

7 Soon after drugs had reached Santa Monica, gang violence grew worse. One evening, Oscar and a group of his friends sat on a corner when a truck loaded with teens stopped in the middle of the street.

8 "Where are you from?" asked a boy from the truck.

9 "We're not in any gang," answered one of Oscar's friends. He knew what the boys were after.

10 A teen in the back of the truck pulled a shotgun out and aimed it at Oscar. "You're lucky," he laughed, and the truck sped off. Some of Oscar's childhood friends haven't been so lucky. Four of

them have been shot to death; another eighteen have been wounded by gunfire. Many more are in jail or on drugs. On any given night, Oscar hears gunshots echo through his apartment complex, as one poor kid tries to gun down another poor kid.

11 Drawn into this world of drugs, violence and gangs, Oscar almost became another victim. "Up through junior high, I was the kind of kid who could have remained a criminal and become a gang member." What saved him, he explains, was the tragic death of his next-door neighbor. Oscar was just 12 when he heard gunshots coming from the street near his home. "We went out to see what happened, and I saw my neighbor lying on the ground. He was only 14, but he was dying." The experience changed Oscar. "Watching what happened to my friend woke me up. I knew I wanted something else for myself, for my friends, and for my community. I just didn't know what to do or where to begin. School was the first place to look."

12 School had always been trouble for Oscar. In kindergarten, because English wasn't his primary language, he had been labeled a "slow learner." This label affected Oscar for years, landing him in the less challenging classes. Since his parents had little understanding of the value or challenges of education, they were unable to help him get the most out of school. During junior high, while he was on the streets with his friends, Oscar's grades went downhill. "I would make it to school only three or four days a week," he explains. "C's and D's, that's where I was. The school suspended me three times." It wasn't until the end of junior high that Oscar's grades recovered.

13 In high school, Oscar got involved with football. "Like most kids, I wanted to be part of something, but instead of joining the gangs that had killed so many of

my friends, I joined the school football team." Being part of the team opened Oscar's eyes to a different way of life. "When I was invited to my teammates' houses for parties, I would be amazed. Here were these big, beautiful houses with swimming pools and saunas. The other guys talked about vacations, about skiing trips. I would say, 'How did you get these things?' and learn that their parents were professional people: doctors, lawyers, accountants. I realized their success came from education." Previously, no one had ever mentioned to him that such career choices were possible or that education could lead to such high positions. In fact, even the school guidance counselor failed to explain to Oscar what he could achieve.

14 "I remember the first time I walked in the office," he says. "The counselor asked me what I wanted to do, and I said 'I don't know.' Then he asked me what my father did, and I said, 'He's a mechanic.' The counselor shuffled some papers and then gave me his professional opinion: 'Why not be a mechanic, too?'"

15 At first, Oscar accepted what the counselor suggested and that college was not an option. The years of watching fellow Mexicans work as house cleaners, farm laborers, and landscapers had convinced Oscar that his career choices were limited to difficult physical labor. "I am Mexican," he thought. "I am not supposed to be able to wear a tie and get a professional job. I am Mexican; all I can do is work with my hands. I am Mexican; I am not as smart as everybody else." The powerful environment of the Corridor had limited Oscar's image of himself.

16 It took time, but Oscar learned to reject the counselor's advice. Sticking with football, he began spending his free time with his family and at church. "In church, as in my family, I learned that yes, I was Mexican and poor, but that I

was also a human being with a heart who was capable of loving and being loved." The combination of family, church, and sports created a force powerful enough to resist the crime and poverty that were right outside his window.

17 With the discipline from football carrying over to his schoolwork, Oscar's grades began to rise from mostly C's to all A's and B's. At the same time, however, gang violence and drugs in the Corridor continued to worsen. When he was 17, another friend was gunned down just up the block from his apartment. Oscar watched as his friend trembled, gasped, and died on the street. Both angered and saddened, Oscar knew what career he wanted to pursue. He vowed to dedicate his life to improving the lives of Mexican-Americans and fighting against the destructive forces in his community. This vow has driven Oscar ever since.

18   In the eleventh grade, an unexpected opportunity came Oscar's way. The ABC news program *20/20* produced a story on education in America. Two schools were featured in the program: one on the East Coast and the other Oscar's school, Santa Monica High School. Santa Monica was chosen because of its size (three thousand students) and diversity°. Oscar was one of the Santa Monica students picked to be interviewed by the program's host, Barbara Walters. "The show chose me because I wasn't in the college-prep program. I didn't look like I was going anywhere. But when they gave me a chance to tell people what it's like here, I had to take it. I told them what it meant to be Mexican in the Corridor and how difficult it is to succeed in a world that teaches you that you are going to be a criminal and that college isn't an option. I explained to them how I had never even been advised to go to college, but instead to learn a trade."

19   Oscar's appearance on the national news program made him an instant celebrity at Santa Monica High. He saw his new popularity as a chance to do what no Latino had done since 1948: become president of the high-school student body. He ran and won.

20   The experience of being elected student body president was exhilarating° for Oscar, and his fellow Mexican-American students were thrilled as well. "It was great for all of us 'underachievers' to work on the campaign," he remembers. "They were proud to see one of their own running for a position of respect. I was also surprised at how many different kinds of people supported me. Blacks and whites, teachers and students—for once, they all came together. Winning that election, and every election I've won since, has assured° me that I am doing what they hope to see done.

They are convinced by my actions that I am helping. I want to show other young Chicanos that there can be more for them than gangs."

Oscar visits with his older brother Agustin, who lives in the Pico Corridor.

21   Oscar used his presidency to bring together different groups in his school. He raised school awareness of what it means to be Mexican-American by organizing *Cinco de Mayo* (fifth of May—Mexican Independence Day) celebrations. He also spoke to school administrators and local police about the problems in the Corridor.

22   That same year, Oscar met with another guidance counselor. This time he was encouraged to go on to college. His grade point average and college entrance exam scores were still too low to qualify him for admission to California State University at Chico, the school he hoped to attend. Fortunately, however, the school offered a summer program called Bridge,

designed to help minority students prepare for college success. If they did well in Bridge, they could be admitted to the university.

23 Oscar entered the Bridge program with a goal. He hoped to prove he was able not only to do college-level work, but to excel°. He succeeded, completing the Bridge program with honors. He then entered the university, earned a B+ grade average his first year, and chose to major in political science. He also continued his involvement in student leadership, becoming the college's first Latino student body president. Since graduating, he has spent a final few months in his neighborhood prior to leaving for graduate school at the University of Texas on a full fellowship.

24 Outside of Oscar's apartment, drugs, gangs, and crime still infect the Corridor. "I've had guns pointed at me and people shot outside my front door. Sometimes my own people question my behavior. When I wear a shirt and tie, they think I am trying to forget my roots in the Corridor," he says, shaking his head. "That's not it at all. They have trouble understanding that to get in a position that can really change things, you have to go to school. But it's even harder with the younger kids," he adds. "When they listen to me telling them how important it is to go to school, they see a man without a car, living in a small apartment. When they listen to gang members telling them to join, they see nice cars, nice clothes, and lots of money. I want them to realize that cars, clothes, and money can be taken away by anyone, but that no one can take away an education."

25 So Oscar doesn't give up. He has started a program with Santa Monica Community College providing young people from the Corridor with special assistance in attending the school. In addition, he takes teenagers from his neighborhood to the campus, showing many of them a college for the first time. He tells them of another way of life besides the violence on the streets. For the several hours that they are with him, they look at classrooms and see students working hard to earn a better life. For several hours, they get away from the graffiti-covered walls, the gunshots, and the sirens. For several hours, they are safe.

26 Walking down the streets of the Corridor, Oscar de la Torre is aware of all the people who are just trying to survive like people everywhere. He reminds himself, "Evil acts do not succeed because of evil men, but because of good men who remain silent."

27 Oscar de la Torre is determined not to remain silent.

Vocabulary Check

1. In which sentence would the word **diversity** make sense?
   a. When it comes to music, I prefer _____ —I listen only to rap.
   b. The _____ of the train passing by makes me want to travel to faraway places.
   c. To be sure you have a balanced diet, eat a _____ of foods.

2. In which sentence would the word **exhilarating** make sense?
   a. It was _____ to watch our football team win their final game of the season.
   b. The _____ experience of having our dog put to sleep left me depressed.
   c. My grandfather is not supposed to do such _____ work as cutting grass.

3. In which sentence would the word **assured** make sense?
   a. The wind _____ through the trees with a whistling sound.
   b. My boss _____ me that I will get a raise in the fall.
   c. The sudden rainstorm _____ us, and we were soaked to the skin within minutes.

Standing behind Oscar are his father, Francisco, and his mother, Candelaria.

4. In the sentence below, the word **primary** means
   a. accidental.
   b. legal.
   c. main.

   "In kindergarten, because English wasn't his primary language, he had been labeled a 'slow learner.'" (Paragraph 12)

5. In the sentence below, the words **prior to** mean
   a. after.
   b. before.
   c. instead of.

   "Since graduating, he has spent a final few months in his neighborhood prior to leaving for graduate school at the University of Texas." (Paragraph 23)

SCORE: (Number correct) _____ x 20 = _____ %

Reading Check

Central Point and Main Ideas

1. What is the central point of the reading?
   a. Oscar has risen above the negative influences of the Pico Corridor and wishes to help others do so too.
   b. An appearance on a national news show made Oscar an instant celebrity at Santa Monica High.
   c. Many young people die because of drugs and gang violence in the Pico Corridor.

2. What is the main idea of paragraph 3?
   a. At the age of 5, Oscar had a bad experience with the police.
   b. Everywhere Oscar went, white people were in higher positions.
   c. Oscar received the message that as a Mexican, he was bad.

3. What is the main idea of paragraph 16?
   a. Oscar continued to play football for his high-school team.
   b. The de la Torres are a religious family who go to church a lot.
   c. Oscar spent his time doing things that helped him resist negative influences.

4. What is the main idea of paragraph 20?
   a. The election motivated and thrilled Oscar and his fellow Mexican-American students.
   b. Many types of people voted for Oscar.
   c. Oscar won the election for the student body presidency as well as other elections.

Supporting Details

5. When Oscar saw two friends try crack cocaine,
   a. he begged for a chance to try the drug too.
   b. he realized he could make a lot of money selling crack.
   c. he refused to try the drug.

6. The first guidance counselor Oscar talked with told him to
   a. go out for football and try to get an athletic scholarship to college.
   b. run for the office of student body president.
   c. be a mechanic like his father.

7. Santa Monica High School was featured on *20/20* because it is
   a. a small, mostly Hispanic school.
   b. an academically outstanding school.
   c. a large school with a varied student body.

Conclusions

8. You can conclude from paragraph 13 that
   a. Oscar began to think that if he got an education, he might someday have a highly respected, well-paid job.
   b. quite a few of Oscar's teammates were also Mexican-Americans.
   c. Oscar was deeply uncomfortable at his teammates' houses and did not like to attend parties there.

9. You can conclude from paragraph 24 that
   a. neighborhood kids see that Oscar is making the right choices for his life.
   b. the crime rate in the Corridor has gone down in recent years.
   c. the attractions of gang life make it hard for Oscar to help kids.

10. You can conclude from paragraph 26 that Oscar believes
    a. anyone who lives in the Corridor is evil.
    b. it is easier to survive in the Corridor than in most other places.
    c. bad situations improve only when people speak up.

SCORE: (Number correct) _____ x 10 = _____ %

Questions for Thinking and Discussion

1. Oscar says that some people expect poor nonwhite kids like those of the Corridor to be criminals and gang members. Why do you think some people have this belief? How can this belief be changed?

Oscar has started a support group for young people from the Corridor who are students at Santa Monica Community College. He meets with them weekly in the library.

*Oscar, his brother Francisco, Jr. (left), and his friend Gordi Barba visit with
Luke Fikaris, a sixth-grade teacher who influenced all their lives.*

2. Some people question Oscar's behavior, saying that Oscar is trying to forget his roots in the Corridor. Why do you think these people act this way? What is it about Oscar that bothers them?

3. As Oscar's experience suggests, we are influenced by what others expect of us. What do your friends, family, and teachers expect of you? Do they expect too much? Too little? Explain.

Ideas for Writing

1. Oscar worries that kids in his neighborhood look at him and at the gang members and decide that it is better to be a gang member. Write a paper for those kids to read. Call the paper "A Vision of the Future." Describe what you think Oscar's future might be like. Then describe what you think the future holds for the gang members. End with a sentence that encourages the kids to follow Oscar's example.

2. Oscar believes we must not remain silent but must do something when we see a bad situation. Write a paper describing a time when someone you know spoke out and acted to correct a wrong.

Kate Vant was a rebellious kid with quick fists and an even quicker mouth. Feeling like a misfit everywhere, she accepted violence as part of her life—until it brought her close to tragedy. Struggling to escape a life of abuse and addiction, she found abilities within herself she never knew existed.

15 / Kate Vant

Words to Watch

factors (3): reasons or influences that contribute to a result
Two *factors* in the new restaurant's success are its reasonable prices and its friendly staff.

preying on (13): making victims of
Older students were *preying on* first and second graders, demanding their lunch money.

accelerated (20): increased
Sun has *accelerated* the aging of my skin.

poring through (29): studying carefully
The sisters spent hours *poring through* their great-grandmother's diary.

geology (30): the study of rocks, minerals, and other parts of the earth
A *geology* expert can tell a lot about an area by looking at its rock formations.

Kate Vant, who is majoring in geology, examines rocks on a hillside near her home.

Ask most people about their earliest memories of school, and they'll mention things like having their own desk, the smell of chalk, learning to read, or making new friends. [1]

Ask Kate Vant about her early memories. She'll tell you about climbing the playground fence and running off to a nearby orchard. There she and her brothers smoked cigarettes and pelted each other with crab apples. As long as she sneaked back into school before dismissal time, her teachers didn't complain much. Kate was only eight years old, but her reputation at her Maryland school was already well established. She was loud-mouthed, wild, and rebellious. Her first school suspension occurred in second grade when Kate ran furiously down the hall, trying to tackle another child who had pushed her. An older student on safety patrol stepped in her way, and Kate sent her flying. "I was a very angry kid," she says today. [2]

What made Kate so angry? Looking back, she identifies several factors°. For one thing, her parents worked long hours. Kate and her twin brothers, Jeff and Mike, who were two years older, were often alone. "We were pretty much on our own from an early age," she says. "We'd get ourselves up and to school, if we went to school at all. A lot of the time we'd just hook." Secondly, the Vants were [3] the only white family in a low-income neighborhood of black and Hispanic people. "We stuck out," Kate says. "We were an easy target, just as a black family in an all-white neighborhood would be. I had some friends who didn't see color, but there were also times when it was black against white, and we were the only whites." Most important, Kate was raised in a family where conflict often turned physical. "My dad is a real likable guy, a peacemaker. Mom was always the disciplinarian, and she tended to be real 'handy,' just as her mom had been. When she needed to discipline us, she'd do it fast and in the old-fashioned way."

4   Unfortunately, the habit of using the hands to express disapproval or settle differences took root among the children. Kate grew up thinking it was normal for brothers and sisters to fight violently and often. Jeff, especially, would hit her hard, leaving her with painful bumps and bruises. The twins seemed to take pride in Kate's toughness. Even when she didn't wish to hurt anyone, they would goad her into fighting other kids. "They'd tell me, 'Beat him up or we'll beat your butt.'"

5   When Kate was in third grade, the family moved to a white area in Bowie, Maryland. Kate didn't know what to make of this new neighborhood and school. She remembers a day when all the students were called to the cafeteria to hear the principal announce that on the next day some "special children" would be joining the school. "The principal said, 'These children are just like you and me, only a little different,'" Kate recalls. She tried to imagine what these "different" children would be like, and finally concluded that they would be physically disabled like the children her mother, a nurse, sometimes cared for.

6   The next day when the new students showed up, Kate looked hard, but couldn't see anything unusual about them. "The teacher called them up one by one and introduced them, and I kept looking around for the wheelchairs and leg braces. After a long time, I realized the 'difference' was that they were black. Like that was a big deal!"

7   Kate tended to play with the black children at least as much as the white. In fact, when the children split into teams for a game, Kate's black friends always invited her to be on their team. She also spent more time with boys than girls. With them she climbed trees, played soccer, and, of course, got into fights.

8   Kate's suspensions continued through sixth grade. When another student challenged her, she'd throw a punch. If a teacher spoke sharply to her, Kate would fly back with a loud, angry retort. If she was sent to the office, she'd leave school and head home. She explains, "I knew I'd be suspended anyway, so what was the point in staying around to be yelled at?"

9   As she grew older, she didn't feel comfortable anywhere. She was a girl who liked to play with boys, a white kid who hung around with blacks, a rebel at school, and a punching bag at home. The fights with her brothers continued and became more serious. After such arguments, she would often have a bloody nose, bruises, black eyes.

10   She didn't think such marks were unusual until other people noticed them. "I came into shop class one day with a real beauty of a black eye, and the teacher said, 'My God, what happened to you?'" Kate recalls. "I said my brother and I had a fight. The teacher advised me that next time, I should pick up a hammer and slam Michael in the head with it. I said, 'That could kill him!' and the teacher responded, 'Well, from the looks of it, that's what he's trying to do to you.'"

11   Kate quit school when she was 15. She got a job at a local fast-food restau-

rant and spent much of her time smoking marijuana. Michael moved away from home soon afterwards, but Jeff was increasingly aggressive, pushing and punching her. A friend of his, Adam, was living with the family. One morning when Kate was late for work, she found Adam locked in the bathroom, taking a shower. She knocked on the door, yelling for him to hurry up. The next thing she knew, Jeff "went ballistic."

12   "He ran into the living room and sent me flying, screaming that I couldn't tell his friends what to do. He punched me, and suddenly I had had enough." Kate left and ran to the house of a friend named Joey. Together they picked up Kate's last paycheck, gathered her clothes, and drove to the bus station in nearby Washington, D.C. There Kate bought a ticket to Arizona, where her Aunt Sally lived.

13   The long bus trip from Washington to Arizona was a wild, sometimes frightening adventure. Although Kate pretended she was merely visiting relatives, it must have been clear from her appearance that she was a runaway. She carried a green plastic garbage bag stuffed with her clothes, her eye was black and swollen, and her bruised ribs slowed her steps. During rest stops along the way, she was an obvious target for men who hung around bus stations, preying on° young runaways. "They were quick," Kate says. "I'd blink my eye, and one would be ten feet closer, checking me out."

14   Avoiding such men was not the only problem. Kate also had a frightening encounter on the bus with a huge, mentally ill woman who decided Kate was in need of salvation—she made Kate kneel in the aisle, muttered some prayers over her, and then angrily insisted that Kate get off the bus. Kate realized she needed protection. "I saw a man and woman and two kids, and I just grabbed the man's arm and said, 'Can I stick with you, please?' Fortunately, they turned out to be really good people." For the rest of the trip, the family watched out for Kate, even staying with her in the Arizona bus station until her cousin arrived to pick her up.

15   Kate liked Arizona. She got along well with her aunt and adored her seven-year-old cousin. Her aunt owned several rental houses, and Kate helped out by keeping them clean and repaired. But after a year, Kate began to think about going back to school—a private school this time. She moved to Maryland, and her parents helped her enroll at St. Vincent School.

16   She nearly made it through the year. She and Jeff avoided one another, and she worked harder in school than she had before. "It was the first time I'd come close to applying myself to my studies, and I tried to keep my mouth shut," she says.

But three days before the year's end, she forgot a textbook she needed to take a final exam. When the dean refused to let her borrow one, she got into a screaming fight with him. He told her to take her exam and then leave the school forever.

17   After that, Kate thought she was finished with school. She began picking up jobs in construction, finding that she had a natural talent for building. At that time, it was a life that suited her. She had money coming in and a crew of workers to hang around with. Their life was pretty simple, revolving around where the party would be tonight, who had gotten drunkest the night before, and who could talk the most crudely. Smoking marijuana and drinking alcohol kept Kate mellow and mindless as she went through the routine of her days.

18   When a new laborer was hired to assist Kate, the two felt an instant attraction. "Kenny was very good-looking, very well-built—the kind of looks that make girls' heads spin off their shoulders," Kate says. Kate and Kenny moved in together almost immediately. They lived in an area called North Beach where there was a community of heavy drug users.

19   Kenny told Kate that he had been in prison. In a barroom fight, he had nearly killed another man by hitting him over the head with a heavy glass. Kate wasn't particularly shocked. "I thought, 'Well, either of my brothers could have gotten in trouble over a bar fight,'" she says. It didn't seem unusual to her either when Kenny began beating her. "It didn't occur to me that there was anything wrong with hauling off and hitting a girl," she remembers. "I'd lived with that all my life."

20   But the abuse soon accelerated° beyond anything Kate had known previously. In her depression and pain, she increased her drug use. At first, she snorted cocaine and took pills. Then her drug supplier threatened to cut her off unless she began mainlining—injecting the drugs with a needle. She resisted the idea briefly, but then gave in to the pressure. With her mind clouded by drugs, she didn't have to think too much about her life and the abuse she was suffering.

21   She tries to explain now why someone like her—in some ways, so tough and self-sufficient—would stay with an abusive partner. "I don't know if anyone can understand who hasn't been abused," she says. "People get so angry at abused women, saying, 'Why do you stay? You must be sick. You must like it.'

22   "Sick, yes. Like it, no. You're convinced that nobody wants you, that nobody but your abuser cares anything about you, that you don't deserve anything but this." Incredibly, after a year of living with Kenny's abuse, she married him. She still hoped that somehow, things would change. "That's how abusers control you—they get you beaten down so low that you're desperate for hope, and you just grab onto any that they offer. He'd always apologize, always promise he would change, always tell me how he wanted us to have a house and kids and be happy together. I wanted to believe him."

23   One night only three weeks after the wedding, Kenny became so violent that Kate was convinced she was going to be killed. She drove frantically to her parents' house, "nearly breaking down their front door with my truck. I just ran in the house and dived into bed between them and lay there shaking."

24   Concerned for her safety, her parents put her on a plane to her aunt in Arizona. She stayed there for a while, moved to New York, then returned to Maryland and obtained a divorce.

25   Once back home, Kate wanted badly to free herself from her drug and alcohol habit. She joined Alcoholics Anonymous.

"I am very grateful to AA," she says today. "They taught me a lot about caring for myself, respecting myself. I had a hard time forgiving myself for some of the things I'd done, but through AA I learned to say, 'OK—I've made some bad mistakes, but that time is done and gone. I'm moving on.'"

26   Although Kate "moved on" from her dependence on drugs and alcohol, the rest of her life seemed stalled. Still working in construction, she had no plans beyond earning a paycheck. She was bored and restless. She was living with a new boyfriend, Irvin, who worked part-time in construction and played in a band.

27   She remembers looking at Irvin one day and having a depressing thought. "He was thirteen years older than me, and it seemed like every time I looked he had lost another tooth," she says. "He couldn't keep a job; he didn't have any real goals. That made me think, 'Well, what about me? I'm also floating from job to job. I'm going nowhere, too.'"

28   She tried to talk about her feelings to Irvin, saying that perhaps she should go to college. He laughed at her. "He said, 'You? You can't put together three sentences. I've never even seen you read a book. What can you do?'" With the old spirit that used to irritate teachers so much, Kate stood up for herself. She said, "Maybe I haven't accomplished much. But I can do better than this."

29   To the astonishment of her parents, Kate left Irvin, moved back home, and enrolled in a basic English course at Prince George Community College. "One course—that's all I tried at first," she says. "I'd been out of school for ten years, and when I was there, I wasn't really there, so I knew it would be hard." And it was. Kate spent hours every day struggling with her assignments, writing and rewriting and poring° through the dictionary. She saw the course as a chance to learn to communicate. "I wanted to be able to talk to people about important things, to express my thoughts, but I really didn't have the vocabulary," she says. "I was very limited in what I could say, and most of my talk was slang." Her instructor, Dr. John McCann, challenged her constantly. "He made me realize how I sounded, not in a mean way, but he wouldn't let me get away with anything," she recalls. "I'd start speaking to him and say, 'Man, you know,' and he'd interrupt and say 'Man? Yes, I'm a man, but what does that mean? And what is it that I'm supposed to know? What do you really want to say to me?'" Gradually, with hard work and Dr. McCann's help, Kate became more skilled in expressing her ideas. "Somehow, through it all, I knew that I was smart," says Kate, "but I sure did need educating. And I still do."

30   Today Kate is a 29-year-old junior at Western Montana College in Dillon. There she has discovered a love for science that has led her to major in geology°. Her dream is to work in a scientific field, perhaps in mining. She still enjoys construction as a hobby, even making her own furniture, but says, "For a career, I want to reach for higher goals."

31   Sometimes she feels discouraged when she observes her younger classmates. "I think, 'Wow, these kids are only 20, and they know so *much*.' But the fact is, they went to school and studied, and I never did. I goofed off, and now I have to catch up."

32   Looking back at her earlier years, she expresses wonder at how far she's come. "I never, never, never thought I could be in college, and doing well. I never could have imagined myself living this life. I like myself and I like what I'm doing. That's a pretty amazing change."

Vocabulary Check

1. In which sentence would the words **preying on** make sense?
   a. The dishonest men were _____ elderly people by selling them worthless health insurance.
   b. On summer evenings, it is pleasant to listen to crickets _____ the twilight.
   c. Volunteers at the soup kitchen are _____ homeless families by serving them a hot lunch every day.

2. In which sentence would the word **accelerated** make sense?
   a. Some drivers _____ their speed when the light turned yellow.
   b. Sadly, the singer's once rich, strong voice has _____ with age.
   c. After my brother gave me the measles, I _____ by giving him the mumps.

3. In the sentence below, the word **pelted** means
   a. hit.
   b. excused.
   c. escaped.

   "She'll tell you about climbing the playground fence and running off to a nearby orchard [where] she and her brothers . . . pelted each other with crab apples." (Paragraph 2)

Kate enjoys making repairs around her house. Here she paints her kitchen ceiling.

4. In the sentence below, the word **goad** means
   a. surprise
   b. forbid.
   c. urge.

   "Even when she didn't wish to hurt anyone, they would goad her into fighting other kids." (Paragraph 4)

5. In the sentence below, the word **retort** means
   a. light-hearted remark.
   b. polite question.
   c. quick, direct answer.

   "If a teacher spoke sharply to her, Kate would fly back with a loud, angry retort." (Paragraph 8)

SCORE: (Number correct) _____ x 20 = _____%

Reading Check

Central Point and Main Ideas

1. What is the central point of the reading?
   a. Because Kate had grown up with violence, she at first accepted the idea that her husband would abuse her.
   b. Kate grew up in a difficult environment and made some poor choices, but she is now making up for lost time as an adult college student.
   c. When children are left on their own too much, as Kate and her brothers were, they are likely to get into trouble.

2. What is the main idea of paragraph 3?
   a. A family that is a different race than most of its neighbors will often be a target for physical and verbal abuse.
   b. There were several reasons why Kate became an angry, aggressive person.
   c. Kate's mother was more likely to discipline the children than her father was.

3. What is the main idea of paragraph 17?
   a. Kate had natural ability as a builder.
   b. The laborers with whom Kate worked held a lot of parties.
   c. Kate cared about little except making a living and getting high.

Supporting Details

4. When Kate went to shop class with a black eye, her teacher
   a. pretended he didn't see her injury.
   b. tried to warn her that her brother could kill her.
   c. took her to the nurse's office.

5. When Kate realized she was in danger on the bus to Arizona, she
   a. asked a family on the bus if she could stay with them.
   b. got off the bus at the next stop.
   c. asked for help from a police officer.

6. After living with Kenny's abuse for a year, Kate
   a. married him.
   b. charged him with assault.
   c. asked him to see a counselor.

7. Irvin played a part in Kate's decision to go to college by
   a. encouraging her to use her mind to improve her situation.
   b. lending her money to enroll in her first course.
   c. being an example for her of someone who lacked goals.

Conclusions

8. You can conclude from paragraph 3 that
   a. Kate's mother was a handy housekeeper.
   b. Kate's mother had a gentle way of disciplining the children.
   c. Kate's mother disciplined the children by hitting them with her hands.

9. You can conclude from paragraph 6 that
   a. Kate was so accustomed to having black friends that she hadn't noticed the new students' color.
   b. the teachers had not realized that the new students were black.
   c. Kate was not used to being in school with black students.

10. You can conclude from paragraph 19 that
    a. if Kate had not lived with violence before, she might have been more alarmed by Kenny's behavior.
    b. before meeting Kate, Kenny had never abused a woman.
    c. one of Kate's brothers had also hit someone over the head with a jar.

SCORE: **(Number correct)** _____ **x 10 =** _____ **%**

Questions for Thinking and Discussion

1. Kate states, "People get so angry at abused women, saying, 'Why do you stay? You must be sick. You must like it.'" Why do you think people sometimes seem angry at abused women? Do you think that is fair? Why or why not?

2. If you were a teacher or principal of an elementary school, how would you react to a "loud-mouthed, wild, and rebellious" student like Kate? Explain two or three methods you would try and what you hope they would achieve.

3. Kate was frequently suspended throughout elementary school. What do you think is the purpose of such suspensions? Do you think most suspensions achieve this purpose? Are there any other ways schools might handle student misbehavior?

Kate studies at her desk at home, preparing for her next day's classes.

*Class over for the day, Kate leaves a building
on the campus of Western Montana College.*

Ideas for Writing

1. When Kate decided to run away, she went to her friend Joey for help. Do you have a friend who has been there for you at a difficult time? Write a paper about that person and how he or she supported you when you needed help.

2. The arguments in Kate's family were dangerous and violent, but all families have conflicts of one kind or another. Think about one such conflict in your family. Write a paper describing the conflict and then explaining what steps everyone involved could take to ease the conflict.

16 / Margaree Crosby

Words to Watch

era (3): period of time known for some type of special events
The beginning of the twentieth century was an *era* of great industrial progress.

particular (6): concerned with details
Our teacher is *particular* about the way her desk is organized.

hostile (7): unfriendly
My former friend gave me a *hostile* look.

retreat (13): turn back
When the burglar heard a growling dog inside, he decided to *retreat*.

indignant (25): angry (at an injustice)
We were *indignant* to learn that the money we gave to charity had been spent on gambling.

Margaree Crosby demonstrates a class activity to students at Clemson University.

Margaree Seawright Crosby was born in 1941 in Greenville, one of the largest cities in South Carolina. She still lives there, but the Greenville of today has little resemblance to the one Margaree grew up in. Today, black and white residents shop in the same stores, eat in the same restaurants, and attend the same schools. That was not the case when Margaree was a young girl.

"The South at that time was a segregated society," Margaree explains. "Segregation affected all aspects of our lives. It meant that blacks and whites could not live in the same area. We couldn't go to the same schools. Hotels were for whites only. We couldn't eat at the lunch counters. We couldn't drink at the same water fountains. Indeed, most places would have two fountains, with a sign saying 'White' or 'Colored' over each one." Margaree and her sisters walked four miles to attend the all-black Sterling High School. "Greenville High School was closer. In fact, we passed it on our way, but we couldn't go there. That was the school for white students."

Margaree Crosby, now a professor at Clemson University in South Carolina, was a pioneer of the civil-rights era°, a time when African-Americans came together to defend their rights as full members of American society. Her life and accomplishments are one small chapter in the story of the black American struggle for complete citizenship.

4 Margaree was one of four daughters born to Mark and Josie Seawright. Her mother worked as a housekeeper for white families in town. While Mark Seawright was in the Navy, his wife and daughters lived in a two-room house. "I remember being taken to the white folks' house where Mama worked," Margaree remembers today. "It seemed so huge!" After Mr. Seawright returned from the military, he went to work in a service station, where he pumped gasoline and washed cars. Mrs. Seawright found a job in a shirt factory, pressing shirts and getting them ready for shipment to stores.

5 Margaree recalls her parents fondly, but differently. "I remember my daddy and granddaddy as both good-humored men, but not the strong influences on me that my mother and grandmother were," she says. "Neither of my parents had gone beyond the eighth grade, but Mama had especially strong values. She was determined to raise us right and to give us the things we needed in life, no matter how hard she had to work." Mr. Seawright left the family when Margaree was 12 and died in an accident when she was an adult.

6 Although the Seawrights were never well-off, Margaree's mother was determined the girls should not feel underprivileged. "We always looked very nice. Mama was particular° about our appearance," Margaree says. "And we had some 'extras' that I can't imagine how she afforded, things like ballet and tap lessons." Margaree's grandmother was a cook at her elementary school. "I was always hanging on her apron strings. Maybe spending all that time around her at the school influenced me to become an educator. I was exposed to all those teachers, who were the most respected women in our community." At that time,

teaching—in blacks-only schools—was one of the very few professions open to Southern black women.

7 As Margaree grew up, she didn't think much about the fact that blacks and whites existed in separate worlds in Greenville. "It was just the way of life," she says. "It was not a hostile° environment. It wasn't as if black people were constantly being insulted on the streets. But we had no interaction with white people. We knew very well not to cross the line." The black children of Greenville knew, for instance, that while they could spend money at the local Woolworth's store, they could not eat at the lunch counter. They could ride the city buses as long as they sat in the back of the bus. They could get an education, but only at the black schools, where they received second-hand textbooks passed down from the white schools. As long as blacks stayed "in their place," life was relatively peaceful.

8 Margaree and her classmates were aware that they did not have the advantages of the local white students, but they were not bitter. "We were very proud of our school, although we knew it wasn't the beautiful school on the hill that the white students went to," she says. "And we had excellent teachers. I regret that I don't remember any of them ever saying, 'We're being treated like second-class citizens. We have to change this.' But we knew we had less because of our color and that we would have to work extra hard to achieve. We knew that education was the key. No one had to tell me to study."

9 One of Margaree's classmates was an ambitious, athletic young man named Jesse Jackson. Jackson later became prominent as a national civil-rights leader and eventually ran for President. Then he was student council president at Sterling High School. His path and Margaree's would cross at other points in their lives.

10   After Margaree graduated from Sterling, she was accepted at South Carolina State College, one of the state's black schools. The college was in the city of Orangeburg, 160 miles from Greenville.

11   As a first-year college student, Margaree began to think more about the conditions blacks lived with in the South. "We students talked together about the way things were," she says. "We could go downtown to Orangeburg to buy things, but that was about it. We couldn't sit down anywhere. We couldn't use the bathrooms, go to the theaters, eat in the restaurants, visit the library. We'd been raised to think the races were 'separate, but equal.' We began to realize that they were separate and *un*equal. Unlike our parents, we reacted to the unfairness of it."

12   The students at South Carolina State began to organize nonviolent protests against segregation in Orangeburg. On several occasions, Margaree and a group of students marched downtown to the Woolworth's store, where they asked to be seated at the lunch counter. Each time, the local police turned the group back.

13   One day, however, the group refused to retreat°. Margaree remembers the day.

14   "The group was very large, much larger than usual," she recalls. "I was wearing a nice coat, trimmed with a raccoon collar. We marched downtown, and as usual, the police ordered us back. This time, we refused. So they turned the fire hoses on us."

15   Horrified, Margaree watched the powerful jets of water striking her friends. Students fell, their bodies spinning on the ground from the force of the water. Some students turned back, but Margaree and many others kept walking. Only when the police sprayed the crowd with tear gas did the students stop their marching.

16   "My beautiful coat was ruined," says Margaree, "and my long hair, which I was always so careful about, was a mess. I felt bad about the way I looked—but I felt good about the statement we had made."

17   News of the South Carolina State students' actions spread throughout the South. At other colleges throughout the region, students held similar protests. "The ripples were spreading," Margaree states. "It was clear the time was past for us to just accept unequal treatment."

18   When Margaree returned home in the summer of 1960 following her first year at college, civil-rights fever was in the air. One evening she, Jesse Jackson, and five other Greenville college students met with the minister of Springfield Baptist Church to plan a protest in Greenville. They decided their target would be the Greenville County Public Library since black Americans were not permitted in the building.

19   "We did have our own library," says Margaree. "It was housed in the Phillis Wheatley Community Center, which was the town's social center for blacks. We loved our library, and we were very proud of it. We had a wonderful librarian, Miss Smith, who was a great encouragement to many of us. But it was very small, just one room, and the books were old. Meanwhile, Greenville County Library was a beautiful two-story building that was supported by tax money—black taxes as well as white."

20   Margaree, Jesse Jackson, and the other five students left the church and walked the six blocks to the library. Trying to appear casual, they walked into the whites-only institution and began looking at books on the shelves.

21   Immediately, the library's director appeared and asked the students to his office. He explained that the black students were not allowed in the building. They responded that the library was a public facility. As college students, they needed the library for research purposes as much as any white students. The director again asked them to leave. Unsure of what to do next, the group did as he asked.

22   The students then returned to the church and talked again with the minister. "He reminded us, 'That library is *yours*,'" Margaree explains. Taking new courage, the group walked to the library again. This time, each of the seven picked a book from the shelf and sat down to read.

23   "I'll never forget—the book I grabbed was something about false teeth," laughs Margaree. "We weren't concerned about what we were going to read, just to read something!"

24   The library director called the police. "A group of big white men in blue uniforms walked in and told us we had to leave. We answered that we were only reading in a public, tax-supported facility.

They told us they would ask us to leave three times, and they did. After the third time, one of them tapped me on the shoulder and said, 'Let's go.'"

During a visit to an elementary school, Margaree reads a story to children.

25   Margaree and her friends were arrested, fingerprinted, and taken to the Greenville jail. She is still indignant° at the memory. "Can you imagine! Arrested for peacefully sitting in a library, reading."

26   At the jail itself, Margaree and her friends were not especially worried. "We weren't too scared because we knew help would arrive soon." Sure enough, two civil-rights attorneys arranged the students' release after several hours in jail.

27   The next day, however, Margaree felt more worried. A picture of the seven students with their names and addresses appeared in the local paper. Margaree and her mother began receiving hate phone calls from angry racists. "We were afraid," she remembers. "My mother didn't criticize me, but I knew she was shocked. We were actually in fear for our lives, and we knew it was because of what I had done."

28   While the students were out on bail, they traveled to a number of churches in

the black community, explaining what they had done and why. Reaction from Greenville residents was at first mixed.

29   "Some of the older people, who had lived with segregation all their lives, had a hard time understanding why we would stir up this trouble," Margaree says. "I could understand their point of view. After all, they were people whose parents and grandparents had to live with the Ku Klux Klan and lynchings. But gradually, most people came around to support us. They realized we were doing what eventually had to be done, not only for us but for the generations to come later."

30   In that summer of 1960, Margaree and the other students eventually appeared in court, where they were supported by strong civil-rights leaders in the community. The judge in the case dismissed all charges against the students. He ordered the doors of Greenville County Public Library opened to the entire community. The students had won.

31   "After the library was integrated, the rest of the city knew it had to fall in line," says Margaree. "It didn't happen overnight, but by 1965 or 1966, the lunch counters, hotels, restaurants, and all the rest of it was pretty well integrated."

32   Margaree returned to South Carolina State, where she graduated with a bachelor's degree in education. She married a fellow student, Willis Crosby, and began teaching school. As the years went by, the couple had three children, and both earned their doctoral degrees from the University of Massachusetts.

33   Dr. Margaree Crosby's adult years have been filled with achievements. She is a full professor of reading and language arts at Clemson University. She introduced the Reverend Jesse Jackson when he spoke there during his campaign for the Democratic presidential nomination in 1984. "That was a special

moment," she remembers. "Jesse and I reminded each other that neither one of us would have been allowed to attend Clemson when we were college students, but here we were." Honors she has received include being profiled by *Jet* magazine and receiving the first South Carolina Women of Achievement award given by the Miss South Carolina Pageant.

34   But the accomplishment that Dr. Crosby speaks of with most satisfaction is her recent appointment as the first female of any race named to the Greenville Hospital Board of Trustees. She recalls a period when, as a 17-year-old high-school student, she was a tray server in the hospital cafeteria. That was as important a hospital job as a black girl could aspire to at the time.

35   When Dr. Crosby was a patient recently at Greenville Hospital, after suffering a mild stroke, she spoke with a young African-American woman, Jennifer Austin, who was cleaning her room.

36   "She'd heard that Jesse Jackson had called me on the phone, and she was curious about me, saying, 'Who are you?' She told me she was 20 years old, had two children, and had her high-school general equivalency diploma. I told her, 'I am so proud of you that you're working here and not sitting at home on welfare. What a good example you're setting for your children.' Then I told her that I used to work in the kitchen of that very hospital.

37   "'You may be cleaning bathrooms now,' I told her, 'but that doesn't have to be your life.'"

38   That young woman's ideas about her future are brighter and more hopeful because of the courage of Margaree Seawright Crosby, Jesse Jackson and other black Americans who stood up with dignity and said, "Enough. We are Americans too. We will have justice."

Vocabulary Check

1. In which sentence would the word **hostile** make sense?
   a. Since my cousin and I argued, we have exchanged _____ letters.
   b. My mother is the kind of _____ person who is always glad to have a guest for dinner.
   c. It was _____ of you to put off doing your term paper until the last minute.

2. In which sentence would the word **indignant** make sense?
   a. Many people are _____ about riding on roller coasters.
   b. That man never keeps a job long because he has such _____ work habits.
   c. Voters were _____ when a candidate lied about his qualifications.

3. In the sentence below, the word **prominent** means
   a. important.
   b. shy.
   c. old-fashioned.

   "Jackson later became prominent as a national civil-rights leader and eventually ran for President." (Paragraph 9)

4. In the sentence below, the word **integrated** means
   a. opened to all races.
   b. closed to the public.
   c. rebuilt from the ground up.

Posing with Margaree are her mother, Josie; her husband, Willis; and her son, Erich.

   "After the library was integrated, the rest of the city knew it had to fall in line." (Paragraph 31)

5. In the sentence below, the words **aspire to** mean
   a. wish for.
   b. reject.
   c. pretend about.

   "That was as important a hospital job as a black girl could aspire to at the time." (Paragraph 34)

SCORE: (Number correct) _____ x 20 = _____ %

Reading Check

Central Point and Main Ideas

1. What is the central point of the reading?
   a. Jesse Jackson was active in civil rights even as a young college student.
   b. Some older black people did not understand why the students were stirring up trouble.
   c. The civil-rights protests of Margaree and others put an end to laws that were unfair to black Americans.

2. What is the main idea of paragraph 7?
   a. Black people had to follow strict rules to get along in Southern society.
   b. The Woolworth stores had lunch counters where only white people could eat.
   c. Black people had to sit in the back of the city buses in Greenville.

3. What is the main idea of paragraph 11?
   a. Margaree and her friends had been raised to think of the races as "separate, but equal."
   b. Black students could shop in downtown Orangeburg, but they could not sit down anywhere.
   c. In college, Margaree and her fellow students became aware of racial injustice.

4. What is the main idea of paragraph 19?
   a. The librarian at the black library encouraged many of Margaree's friends.
   b. The library for white people in Greenville was better than the one for black citizens.
   c. The library in the Phillis Wheatley Community Center filled just one room.

Supporting Details

5. When Margaree was very young, the most respected black women in the community were
   a. school cooks.
   b. teachers.
   c. civil-rights leaders.

6. The textbooks used in Margaree's school came from
   a. donations by local families.
   b. black families living in the North.
   c. white schools which were finished with them.

7. When the students refused to turn back from the Woolworth's store, local police
   a. admitted them to the store's lunch counter.
   b. called the National Guard.
   c. turned on fire hoses against them.

8. When Margaree and her friends were out on bail, they
   a. spoke in local black churches.
   b. left town in fear for their safety.
   c. continued protesting at the public library.

Conclusions

9. You can conclude from paragraph 22 that
   a. it didn't take much courage to go back to the library to sit down and read.
   b. the minister did not really want the students to return to the library.
   c. the minister inspired the students to keep protesting at the library.

10. You can conclude from paragraph 33 that
   a. when Margaree was a college student, Clemson University was for whites only.
   b. Jesse Jackson graduated from Clemson University.
   c. the South Carolina Women of Achievement Award is for blacks only.

SCORE: (**Number correct**) _____ x 10 = _____%

Questions for Thinking and Discussion

1. In order to protest the whites-only policy at the public library, Margaree and the other students quietly walked in and started reading. What might have happened if they had protested in a violent manner?

2. At first, some of the older people in the black community felt it was unwise to protest segregation. Why do you think they felt that way? Why do you suppose Margaree and her friends held such a different point of view?

Margaree reaches for a book in her office at Clemson University.

Margaree has gotten together with Jennifer Austin, the young woman she met while in the hospital, to give her career advice.

3. Despite growing up poor in a segregated society, Margaree has achieved an admirable career. What experiences in her life do you think helped her get so far?

Ideas for Writing

1. Margaree and her fellow protesters were criticized by some older black people for "stirring up trouble." Write a paper defending Margaree's actions. Or if you agree that the students should not have been "stirring up trouble," write a paper defending that view.

2. In talking to each other, the students at South Carolina State College began to see segregation more clearly. What helpful talk have you had with a parent, relative, teacher, or friend? Write a paper in which you explain how talking with someone helped you understand and deal with a specific problem.

School—what a drag! In school, Grant Berry was expected to read, but he would rather sit and watch Fred Flintstone or Gilligan than open a book. Later, parties and girls caught Grant's attention, but school still did not. How did a guy like Grant end up enrolling in college at the age of 27? Read his story to find out.

17 / Grant Berry

Words to Watch

endured (4): put up with
I *endured* the dog's barking all last night, but I am going to speak to its owner today.

vague (6): not clear
Since I had only a *vague* understanding of our science chapter, I decided to read it again.

philosophy (7): set of values and beliefs
A good *philosophy* is to treat everyone with kindness and respect.

evaporated (12): disappeared
Support for the mayor *evaporated* after he was accused of theft.

absorbed (22): taken in; understood
Because I was tired, I *absorbed* little of what the speaker said.

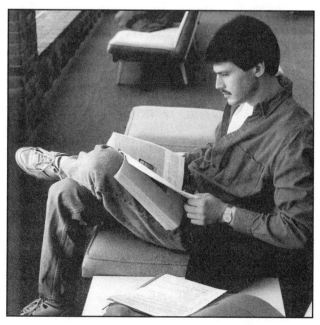

Grant Berry looks over a book before class.

I can remember how the veins popped out on Mrs. Lingstrom's forehead when she got angry. Mrs. Lingstrom was my first-grade teacher. She often did get angry as she tried to stop me from talking and clowning with my best buddy. My best friend was Jack Baun. The class was arranged alphabetically, so "Baun" and "Berry" sat next to one another.

One of the games that Jack and I invented was trying to be the last ones on the playground when recess ended. We succeeded so well that we were sometimes late to class and had to go to the office. While I remember all the horseplay I did in first grade, I don't remember learning much about how to read. Mrs. Lingstrom introduced us to the "letter people"—all the letters of the alphabet—but I don't remember her introducing the letter people to each other so they could form words.

I probably learned to read because my parents read little-kid books to me. To their credit, they were willing to read whenever I waved a book at one of them. Sometimes Dad will still recite from one of my favorites: "I'm a rootin', tootin' cowboy and my name is Cowboy Dan. I can ride 'em, rope 'em, wrangle as good as any man." Both my parents say it got so they could read that book to me without even glancing at the page. However, when I outgrew my parents' laps, I never grew into the habit of reading for myself, except when forced. Clicking on shows about Fred Flintstone, George Jetson, and Gilligan was easier than turning pages.

4   Nobody in my family objected to my choices. In the world I grew up in, school was a place you had to go. But that was it. You went. You endured° it. You stuck it out long enough to get that high-school diploma so you could get a decent job. And then, of course, you never went near a school again.

5   That was the attitude my parents held, especially my father. For my dad, school was the worst kind of prison. He'd graduated from high school, found a factory job making car parts, and has stayed there until this day. He's a good man, and I love him very much. I respect him for being a responsible husband and father. Seldom if ever did he miss a day of work, and he never left his paycheck at a bar. He took his family to church every Sunday, didn't light up or lift a glass, and has celebrated his silver wedding anniversary with his first and only wife. However, if he ever had a dream of being more than a factory worker, I never heard about it.

6   Looking at him, I had a vague° notion that I wanted more out of life. I imagined myself wearing a suit and tie and carrying a briefcase, not working in a factory. Unfortunately, that was as far as my vision went. What I was going to be doing as I wore that suit, and how I was going to get there, was too much trouble to think about.

7   It never occurred to me that school could play a role in helping me realize my dreams. School was a joke, a game. You played the game because you had to, but you certainly didn't take it seriously. One incident that occurred in third grade helped convince me that school just wasn't important. My teacher, Mrs. Harrington, was trying hard to get me to pay attention in class. But all I wanted to do was draw cartoons on the pad of paper I carried everywhere. When Mrs. Harrington contacted my parents, they took my side. "You're not doing anything wrong," they told me. "Your teacher has a problem." Looking back, I realize how much I needed them to crack down on me and support my teacher. I wish they had said to me, "Grant, if you're drawing in class instead of doing your work, you deserve to be in trouble." But their philosophy° was that as long as I got by in school, that was good enough.

8   The pattern for my years in school was set. I worked just hard enough to get by. I don't know how my teachers could have respected themselves after passing me from one wasted class to another.

9   There was just one exception—an English class I took when I was in ninth grade. We did a lot of writing there, and I

was surprised to find out that I enjoyed writing. Even more surprisingly, my teacher seemed to like what I wrote. Once we were assigned to write about someone we wanted to be. I wrote that I wanted to be Hugh Hefner, the publisher of *Playboy* magazine, and I described what I thought life would be like surrounded by all those women. The teacher laughed a lot at what I had written. She told me she would save the piece to use as an example for other courses she taught. That felt pretty good.

10 But that bit of success didn't exactly transform my attitude. In fact, as I grew older and more interested in partying, girls, beer, and cigarettes, I had less interest in school than ever. During my senior year, I met Kathy. We worked in the same grocery store. She was a couple of years older than I, and there were no restrictions on her activities. I tried to keep pace with her lifestyle. We would stay out partying until 3:00 a.m., and then I would sleep through class or not show up at all.

11 My poor attendance became such a problem that the school sent letters to my parents telling them that I would not graduate if I didn't show up for class once in a while. I managed to squeak through the rest of the year, even though I don't remember doing much homework. Yet in June, the principal shook my hand and forked over a diploma. I took it, grinning, and marched in a smug way across the stage. Altogether, high school was a forgettable experience. If it wasn't for my diploma and senior pictures, there would not be enough evidence to convince a jury that I was guilty of having attended at all.

12 With school finally over, I felt I was free. But free for what, I soon began to wonder. I began dreaming about being a disc jockey and signed up for a college broadcasting class. However, my high-school habits came along with me. I rarely did my homework. I frequently forgot to attend at all. And when I learned

that Kathy was pregnant, my tiny surviving interest in school evaporated° completely. We got married, rented an apartment, and settled in for family life.

13 Working as a grocery bagger wasn't going to support a family, so I began looking for something else. I didn't have to look very far. I got an offer to train as a butcher in the same grocery store where I worked. "Learn the butcher's trade, and you'll never need another one," someone told me, and that sounded good to me. I've been a butcher ever since.

14 It isn't a bad job. It certainly has more variety than my father's job, which involves filling and emptying the same machine over and over. I do something different all the time—cut pork chops, chicken, rump roast; give customers advice on how to cook a particular cut of meat. I don't wear a suit and tie—in fact, I'm strapped into a bloody apron and holding a knife—but it's a decent way to make a living.

15 Even with my new job, Kathy and I realized we needed more money. So when my wife's cousin offered us a way to make a second income, I said, "How soon can we start?" The job was selling home products and recruiting others to do the same. To my dismay, he reached into his briefcase and emerged with a stack of books. He explained that to succeed in business, we needed the proper mental attitude. "Read these!" he said, thrusting the stack into my hands.

16 Read these? Me, read these books? I'd done my time! I'd gone through twelve years of school! I thought the deal was that I would never have to read anything again. If this guy wanted me to develop a good attitude, giving me books was having the opposite effect. However, I wanted to make some extra cash, so I reluctantly promised to try.

17 I started reading the books at night, at first with all the enthusiasm of a kid

taking castor oil. I soon became really interested. They were self-help, positive-thinking, self-confidence books. They opened up my world. They told me that I had the potential to achieve great things. I sucked in their message like an old Chevrolet being pumped full of premium gas. It felt so good that I started reading more. Not only did I read at night, but I read during my breaks, at lunch hour, waiting for traffic lights to turn green, and in the bathroom.

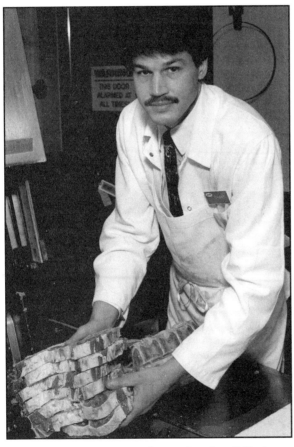

Grant continues to work as a butcher full-time.

18   The home-products business didn't last long, but my newfound passion for reading did. I laid aside the self-help books and began reading whatever I wanted. I got my first library card. I subscribed to *Sports Illustrated*. I found books of short stories and dove into poems. I read countless newspaper articles, cereal boxes, and oatmeal packages.

I was amazed at the riches that were available to me just for the reading.

19   Reading moved me, occasionally to the point that it was a little awkward. For instance, as I read in a crowded lunchroom one day, I stumbled across the story of a young Romanian girl who was saved from starvation by a couple from the United States. I had to jerk the magazine to my face to conceal my tears as I read how she entered her new home, which was filled with toys and stuffed animals.

20   Reading not only tugged at my emotions, but also inspired me to make a move. I remembered those times in high school when I had been praised for my writing, and I knew I wanted to learn to write better. I took a look at my life and realized that college was what I needed.

21   My decision to return to college received mixed responses. Kathy was supportive of the idea. My mother didn't say much. Dad was more outspoken, but no more encouraging. "Send me anywhere, but don't send me back to school" were his words on the subject.

22   At the age of 27, I enrolled at Muskegon Community College. I started out with a pair of English courses and was amazed to find how little I had absorbed° in high school. I hardly knew a comma from a prepositional phrase, and I had no idea what made the difference between a compound sentence and a complex one.

23   Even so, I plunged ahead, determined not just to "get by" this time, but to do my best. And eventually my teachers began to notice my work. One day, my English instructor called me into her office and told me about an essay contest sponsored by a textbook company. She encouraged me to write the story of how I'd turned from a poor student into a good one.

24   After writing and revising the essay four times, in longhand, I felt ready to send it in. When I learned I had won the

third-place award and $500 in the contest, I was so excited I called everybody in the world. Then I took the award money and bought a word processor. My career as a writer had begun.

25 A lot has happened in the last couple of years. Working full time, taking two classes most terms, and raising a family (we have two daughters, Hillary and Natalie) leaves me little free time. Sadly, Kathy and I are separated now, but she's continued to support my educational and career goals. We both encourage our girls to look at school as a wonderful opportunity, and they love their first- and fourth-grade classes. I write a column for the Fruitport, Michigan, newspaper, and I've seen other writing of mine published in the Muskegon Community College literary magazine, a devotional booklet, and a college textbook.

26 I feel that I'm on my way to reaching my ultimate goal: to write books of brief, humorous stories about small-town life and then travel around the country to promote them.

27 Maybe that seems like an impossible dream, but why not? I was a high-school goof-off who turned into a butcher, and a family man who turned into a college student and published writer. Why not believe I can turn into something else—a successful author?

28 The first books I ever read willingly told me, "You can be anything you like as long as you believe in yourself." Their message helped get me where I am today. I continue to believe.

In the college computer lab, Grant works on a paper.

Vocabulary Check

1. In which of the following sentences would the word **endured** make sense?
   a. Our teacher _____ to the class that she had once been labeled a "slow learner."
   b. I have _____ my sister's many unusual pets, but I put my foot down when she said she wanted a large, hairy spider.
   c. Our friends organized a party and _____ our move into a new home.

2. In which of the following sentences would the word **absorbed** make sense?
   a. Interesting lectures are _____ more easily than boring ones.
   b. I _____ the indoor plants onto the patio over the summer.
   c. Traffic was so bad that we could have _____ our way home faster by walking.

3. In the sentences below, the word **transform** means
   a. follow.
   b. explain in detail.
   c. greatly change.

   "But that bit of success didn't exactly transform my attitude. In fact, . . . I had less interest in school than ever." (Paragraph 10)

Spending time with his daughters, Hillary and Natalie, is very important for Grant.

4. In the sentences below, the word **smug** means
   a. self-satisfied.
   b. angry.
   c. sad.

   ". . . in June, the principal shook my hand and forked over a diploma. I took it, grinning, and marched in a smug way across the stage." (Paragraph 11)

5. In the sentence below, the word **emerged** means
   a. left.
   b. came out.
   c. read.

   ". . . he reached into his briefcase and emerged with a stack of books." (Paragraph 15)

SCORE: **(Number correct)** _____ x 20 = _____%

Reading Check

Central Point and Main Ideas

1. What is the central point of the reading?
   a. Grant grew up in a family that did not encourage him to do his best in school.
   b. Grant found that a grocery bagger did not earn enough money to support a family, so he learned to be a butcher.
   c. After years of thinking that school and books were a waste of time, Grant learned to value education and reading.

2. What is the main idea of paragraph 5?
   a. Grant's father didn't like school, but he graduated from high school.
   b. Grant's father is a good, hard-working man who never wanted to be more than a factory worker.
   c. Grant's father has held the same job since he graduated from high school.

3. What is the main idea of paragraph 7?
   a. In third grade, Grant enjoyed drawing cartoons on a pad of paper he carried with him.
   b. Grant's third-grade teacher tried hard to get him to pay more attention in class.
   c. Grant felt school was not important, and his parents encouraged that belief.

Supporting Details

4. Although Grant's parents did not emphasize education, they did
   a. read to Grant when he was a child.
   b. insist Grant stop drawing pictures in class.
   c. want Grant to go to college.

5. The one activity Grant enjoyed in ninth grade was
   a. math.
   b. writing.
   c. singing in choir.

6. In high school, Grant
   a. started studying more.
   b. partied a lot.
   c. failed to graduate.

7. Once he began reading the books his wife's cousin gave him, Grant
   a. decided to quit college.
   b. began a successful career in sales and recruiting.
   c. found he loved to read.

Conclusions

8. You can conclude from paragraph 9 that
   a. Grant's ninth-grade essay was written in a humorous way.
   b. Grant had often been told by other teachers that he was a good writer.
   c. Grant was embarrassed by his teacher's attention.

9. You can conclude from paragraph 17 that
   a. from the start, Grant was enthusiastic about reading.
   b. Grant was not enthusiastic about reading at first.
   c. Grant never became enthusiastic about reading.

10. You can conclude from paragraph 25 that
    a. Grant's daughters are both excellent writers.
    b. as a result of their separation, Grant and Kathy are no longer on speaking terms.
    c. Grant is pleased that his daughters don't have the same attitude towards school that he did at their age.

SCORE: (Number correct) _____ x 10 = _____%

Questions for Thinking and Discussion

1. What could Grant's parents have done to help Grant develop a better attitude towards education?

2. "I don't know how my teachers could have respected themselves after passing me from one wasted class to another," writes Grant. What does he mean by this statement? What do you think he wishes the teachers had done instead?

3. Like Ben Carson, whose story appears on page 167, Grant was surprised to discover that reading was more than something he had to do in school. He found that reading could be a source of great pleasure and could even teach him things he wanted to know. Outside of your schoolbooks, what do you read? What do you like to read about? What are some of the best things you've ever read?

Ideas for Writing

1. Grant's goal is to write and sell humorous books. To reach that goal, he works hard in school and at his writing. Write a paper about a goal you would like to reach. You may write about the kind of work you would like to do in the future. Or you may write about a goal you would like to achieve now—for example, to do well in a certain course, to control your temper, or to develop a better relationship with some member of your family. Describe the goal, and explain in detail one or two things you can do to reach that goal.

2. Grant was amazed when he discovered that he actually enjoyed reading. Write a paper about a time that you, too, found out you liked something or someone you had previously disliked. Explain how and why you changed your mind.

As a young child, Catina Washington was responsible for the care of a baby sister and a mother who could not help herself. When the family was homeless and hungry, it was Catina who had to take charge. The energy that took Catina through those dark times is now helping her climb as high as her dreams can take her.

18 / Catina Washington

Words to Watch

brisk (2): quick and full of energy
The doctors' *brisk* teamwork saved the child's life.

negotiate (12): bargain
Teenagers often try to *negotiate* for a later curfew.

flourished (24): did very well
The dog had been mistreated, but he *flourished* in his new home.

knack (24): talent
Some people have a *knack* for making friends.

prestigious (31): greatly respected
The Heisman Trophy is one of the most *prestigious* awards in football.

Catina Washington looks up from her desk at her job in the School of Business at Tuskegee University.

The voice of the woman on the phone was shaking, desperate. "I spent the night on the street," she said. "I don't have anyplace to go. I got cut up a little. What am I gonna do?"

On the other end of the hotline, Catina Washington went into action. Her voice was brisk° but compassionate. "Where are you right now, sweetie? Have you got bus fare? How bad are you hurt? You stay right there near that phone booth. We're going to figure something out."

During the next hour, Catina moved like a whirlwind. A series of calls to homeless shelters in the Oakland, California, area turned up an available bed. But it was many blocks across town. The woman had only thirty-five cents. And it was getting late—the shelters were closed for the night.

Other hotline volunteers might have told the woman that she needed to make do for the night, that she could go to a shelter in the morning. Not Catina. She dialed her aunt's number. "Auntie Inez," she said, "I've got a big favor to ask."

Within minutes, Catina and her aunt were driving into one of the roughest sections of East Oakland, where they found the woman waiting on a corner. They took her to a shelter, and Catina sweet-talked the director into bending the rules and admitting the woman after hours. Then she gave the woman the two dollars she had in her pocket, said a prayer with her, and went home. "I apologized for not staying longer with her," said Catina, "but I had to get up for high school the next morning."

6   Catina was well known as one of the most dedicated volunteers at the OCCUR (Oakland Citizen's Committee for Urban Renewal) homeless hotline. Her policy was never to go home from her shift until she found shelter for a caller. The people she aided knew she was a loving, energetic young woman with a drive to help the homeless.

7   What they didn't know was that she had once been one of them.

8   Catina started life as the daughter of an unmarried 17-year-old, Judy, whom Catina describes as "slow." "My mother went through third grade and was then put in special classes," she says. "After that, she never went to school much."

9   When Catina was born, Judy turned to her sister Inez for help. "She was scared and didn't know what to do," Catina says. "Auntie Inez told her, 'I'll watch the baby for you and send you to the Job Corps to get some training so you can get on your feet.' So Mom went off, supposedly to school." After that, no one heard from Judy for years.

10   Catina lived with her Aunt Inez and Uncle Wilbert, who had no children of their own, until she finished second grade. Then Judy reappeared, pregnant again, and demanded Catina back. "She said Inez had taken me from her," Catina remembers with some sadness. "It wasn't true, and we even went to court over it, but in those days, it seemed that judges always said a child belonged with its mother, even if the mother wasn't able to care for it."

11   After the court ruled in Judy's favor, Catina and her baby sister set out with their mother on a two-year journey. The trip took them, first, to the state of Washington, then to Louisiana where Catina's grandmother was dying, next to Florida, and finally back to Oakland, where a boyfriend of Judy's had promised the family an apartment.

12   But there was no apartment and no money except for Judy's welfare check. The family headed to the Sutter Hotel, the cheapest place they knew of. It was eight-year-old Catina's job to go into the hotel and negotiate° with the owner over how long the family could stay there.

13   "It was really fortunate that I'd had those early years of schooling," Catina says. "Mom couldn't really read or write, and if she'd tried to handle it, the hotel man would have taken our money and had us out in two days. But he saw that I had some sense and didn't try to cheat me."

14   Once the family settled in a room at the hotel, Catina began hunting for food. She convinced the man at the store across the street to accept food stamps in exchange for groceries. The Salvation Army down the street provided a box of food, mostly condensed tomato soup. Back in their hotel room, Catina and Judy mixed the soup with hot tap water for their meals.

15   Their days revolved around the schedule of the local soup kitchens. Catina remembers that "the one at St. Vincent's Catholic Church was open from 11:00 a.m. to 1:00 p.m. In the afternoon, there was one at the Presbyterian church."

16   When Judy's welfare check ran out, the family was evicted from the hotel. Catina went back to the Salvation Army for help. There were no rooms available. For the next four days, the family hung around the lobby of the Sutter Hotel during the daytime, trying not to be noticed. When night fell, they walked down the street to stand in the entrance of the Salvation Army with other homeless people.

17   Eventually, the family found an apartment where they stayed for six months, still eating their meals in soup kitchens. The building they lived in was grim. "It just got worse and worse," Catina says. "Drug people hanging around, people beating on their wives. Fortunately, I was in school most of the day. But I was really worried about my baby sister, Tanya, who spent her whole day there." To get Tanya out of that environment, Catina took her to the library in the evenings and read to her.

18   Then Aunt Inez found the family.

19   "I came home one day to find her sitting there," Catina says. "She was looking around at the apartment—one room, with a walk-in closet and a bathroom, not even a kitchen, and she said, 'Judy, you have got to let us help you.'"

20   For a while, things seemed to be looking up. Inez found the family a pleasant apartment, bought them some furniture, and found Judy a job at a daycare center. At Catina's urging, Judy signed up for a literacy course, but she soon stopped attending classes. Catina began to lose patience when Judy's new boyfriend moved into the one-bedroom apartment. He disliked the fact that Catina spoke like an educated person, and he didn't mind saying so. "He'd put his feet up on the furniture and say, 'Your daughter—why she talk so prissy? She think she better than us.'" It was at that point, in the summer before sixth grade, that Catina decided she had to act to save herself.

21   "Mom and I were on our way to the mall one Saturday. That's what we'd do, just go and hang out. She never acted the mom role, you know. She was more like a sister or a friend," explains Catina. "That can be nice, but sometimes you want a mother to be a mother, not just a hanging buddy.

22   "So I said to my mother, 'Look, I think it would be better for both of us if I went to stay with Auntie Inez until I finish school.'" This time, Catina's mother agreed and also allowed Tanya to move to Florida to live with her father's family.

23   Moving back in with Inez did not immediately make Catina's life easy. The young girl had plenty of anger and resentment hidden under her calm surface. "We had some rough times at first," Catina explains. "Auntie would tell me to do some little chore, and I'd just blow up. I'd say, 'Why should I? I've been *doing* my whole life. I'm *tired* of doing.'" Inez took Catina to a family counselor. "We got a lot of feelings out," Catina says. "It was the best thing we could have done." Gradually, Catina learned to accept the realities of her life and to return her aunt's love and trust.

24   Once she felt secure in her new environment, Catina flourished°. She enjoyed her years in junior high, and by the time she was in high school, she had become

an excellent student. There, she signed up for ROTC (Reserve Officer Training Corps). She discovered she loved the competition and discipline of military training. And the ROTC classes helped her develop her knack° for public speaking. By the time Catina graduated from high school, she was the highest-ranking female ROTC officer in her school.

Before a finance class, Catina and two classmates page through the Wall Street Journal.

25 During her high-school years, Catina was in touch now and again with her mother. It became important to Catina that Judy attend her high-school graduation. "I wanted her to know that I'd made it that far," she says. She wasn't sure until graduation day whether she would get her wish, but there Judy was, looking pretty in a new dress and shoes that Inez had bought for her. "She was really happy for me and proud that I was going on to a wonderful college," Catina recalls.

26 That college is Tuskegee University in Tuskegee, Alabama. Catina is studying finance and planning to attend law school. Her hard work, devotion to the homeless, and public speaking skills have gained her some impressive honors. She has been featured on Oakland-area talk shows and was named "The Woman of the Year for Northern California" and "One of the Most Caring Students in America."

27 But Catina learned about one of her most surprising honors when her aunt called her from Oakland. "Catina!" she said. "I don't know what this is about, but there's a message on the answering machine saying that Bill Cosby wants you on his TV show!"

28 "You're playing with me," responded Catina in disbelief.

29 But it was true. Bill Cosby was then hosting a game show called *You Bet Your Life*. His producers had contacted Tuskegee University to ask about Catina, whom they had learned about through the honors she had received. After some interviews with the show's producers, Catina was flown to Philadelphia to tape an appearance on the show.

30 "It was a wonderful, amazing experience," Catina reports. "My partner on the show was an 81-year-old weightlifter, and we had a riot together. I got to visit Philadelphia, meet Bill Cosby, and win $683!"

31 Prestigious° awards, television appearances, celebrities—who could have predicted such a future for a homeless little girl? The hardships and responsibilities she had to bear at a young age could easily have destroyed her dreams. Instead, she achieved and continues to achieve more than many born to lives of comfort and security. When asked where her courage and drive come from, her usually rapid-fire speech becomes slower and more thoughtful.

32 "I guess I just looked at the people around me," Catina says, "and I realized

that if I didn't take charge of my life, I would end up like them. I'd be a statistic, another person who didn't make it."

33   Making it matters to her not just for herself, but for others. Catina wants her mother to know that she has "a good kid." She wants her Aunt Inez to feel that the sacrifices she made for Catina were worthwhile. She wants to continue to serve as a role model for her younger sister. And she hopes that her story will encourage other youngsters with difficult lives.

34   "Young people who've had hard times may not believe that there's anything better on the other side of those experiences," Catina says. "I'm here to tell them, 'If you sit back and act like your circumstances can keep you down, you'll stay stuck right where you are. But if you figure out what you have to do and just do it, you *can* change your life.'"

Vocabulary Check

1. In which sentence would the word **negotiate** make sense?
   a. Before I went car shopping, I read an article on how to _____ with salespeople.
   b. The worst thing about my brother is that he will never _____ he's made a mistake.
   c. I cannot _____ the smell of cigarette smoke in a closed room.

2. In which sentence would the word **prestigious** make sense?
   a. The family gathered at Thanksgiving and enjoyed a _____ meal.
   b. Several students got together last night to study for the _____ final.
   c. She was delighted when her granddaughter won a scholarship to a _____ college.

3. In the sentence below, the word **policy** means
   a. excuse.
   b. substitute.
   c. guiding rule.

   "Her policy was never to go home from her shift until she found shelter for a caller." (Paragraph 6)

With her boyfriend, Earl Marks, Jr., Catina walks a campus path.

4. In the sentences below, the word **grim** means
   a. too large.
   b. dirty.
   c. frightening.

   "The building they lived in was grim. 'It just got worse and worse,' Catina says. 'Drug people hanging around, people beating on their wives. . . . I was really worried about my baby sister. . . .'" (Paragraph 17)

5. In the sentence below, the word **circumstances** means
   a. good luck.
   b. situation.
   c. dreams.

   "I'm here to tell them, 'If you sit back and act like your circumstances can keep you down, you'll stay stuck right where you are. . . .'" (Paragraph 34)

SCORE: **(Number correct)** _____ x 20 = _____%

Reading Check

Central Point and Main Ideas

1. What is the central point of the reading?
   a. Catina is grateful that she is no longer homeless.
   b. Catina turned a difficult life into one of achievement and concern for others.
   c. Teenage mothers and their children often end up homeless, just like Judy and Catina.

A picture on Catina's bureau features (left to right) her Aunt Linda and Aunt Inez.

2. What is the main idea of paragraph 5?
   a. Catina did everything she could to help the homeless woman.
   b. Catina knew how to get around the rules at the shelter.
   c. Catina and her aunt were afraid to drive into East Oakland at night.

3. What is the main idea of paragraph 24?
   a. Catina finally felt secure at home with her aunt and uncle.
   b. Catina developed skill in public speaking.
   c. After adjusting to a new life, Catina did very well in school and ROTC.

4. What is the main idea of paragraph 33?
   a. Catina wants to succeed for herself and for others.
   b. Catina wants her mother to know that Catina turned out well.
   c. Catina wants to be a good role model for her younger sister.

Supporting Details

5. Just before sixth grade, Catina went to live with
   a. her aunt.
   b. her grandmother.
   c. her sister.

6. As a child, Catina ate a lot of meals in
   a. the homes of her friends.
   b. local soup kitchens.
   c. the home of her church's minister.

7. While in the ROTC (Reserve Officer Training Corps), Catina discovered that
   a. she did not like military training.
   b. she had a talent for public speaking.
   c. she needed help in several of her classes.

8. One of Catina's most surprising honors was
   a. appearing on TV with Bill Cosby.
   b. winning a trip to Disney World.
   c. being named Tuskegee's Student of the Year.

Conclusions

9. You can conclude from paragraph 25 that
   a. Catina wanted her mother to be proud of her.
   b. Catina was ashamed of Judy.
   c. Judy did not care what happened to Catina.

10. You can conclude from paragraph 29 that
    a. Bill Cosby is still hosting the game show called *You Bet Your Life.*
    b. the show found Catina interesting enough to be a contestant.
    c. Catina did not really want to go on the show.

SCORE: (Number correct) _____ x 10 = _____%

Questions for Thinking and Discussion

1. When Judy wanted to get Catina back from Inez, the judge said that a child belonged with its mother. Do you agree with the judge that a child is always better off with a parent? If you had been the judge, what would you have decided, and why?

2. The summer before sixth grade, Catina felt "she had to act to save herself." From what problems did she want to save herself? How did living with Aunt Inez help Catina solve her problems?

3. Why do you think Inez did so much for Judy and Catina? Do you know any people like Inez? What have they done?

Catina and her roommate, Yvonne Harris, talk in their house.

Ideas for Writing

1. Write a letter to the host of a talk show, like *The Oprah Winfrey Show*, and explain why Catina should be a guest on the program. Tell why her story would interest and help TV viewers.

2. Catina is a determined person who has taken charge of her life. Write a paper about someone you know who is equally strong-willed. Give at least one example of this person's determination.

Ben Carson was convinced he was "the dumbest kid in fifth grade." His report card seemed to say so, too. Then Ben's mother came up with a simple plan that changed his life. Today Ben Carson is a world-famous surgeon at Johns Hopkins Hospital in Baltimore, Maryland. This chapter from his autobiography Think Big *tells how a "dummy" became a brilliant student.*

19 / Benjamin Carson, M.D.

Words to Watch

inasmuch as (13): because
Inasmuch as there was only one candidate, everyone knew who would win the election.

trauma (20): emotional pain
The shooting of the president caused much *trauma* throughout the nation.

consequently (20): as a result
The temperature fell to 50 degrees overnight; *consequently*, we did not go swimming.

rebellious (46): defiant; resisting authority
My cat isn't allowed on the dining table, but when he feels *rebellious,* he sits there anyway.

astonished (81): surprised
My sister was *astonished* to learn that she had been adopted.

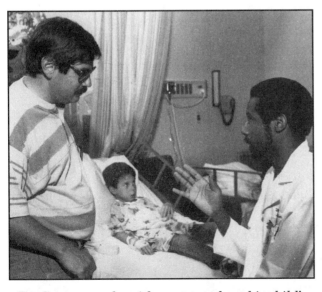

Dr. Carson speaks with a parent about his child's medical condition.

"**B**enjamin, is this your report card?" my mother asked as she picked up the folded white card from the table. [1]

"Uh, yeah," I said, trying to sound unconcerned. Too ashamed to hand it to her, I had dropped it on the table, hoping that she wouldn't notice until after I went to bed. [2]

It was the first report card I had received from Higgins Elementary School since we had moved back from Boston to Detroit, only a few months earlier. [3]

I had been in the fifth grade not even two weeks before everyone considered me the dumbest kid in the class and frequently made jokes about me. Before long I too began to feel as though I really was the most stupid kid in fifth grade. Despite Mother's frequently saying, "You're smart, Bennie. You can do anything you want to do," I did not believe her. [4]

No one else in school thought I was smart, either. [5]

Now, as Mother examined my report card, she asked, "What's this grade in reading?" (Her tone of voice told me that I was in trouble.) Although I was embarrassed, I did not think too much about it. Mother knew that I wasn't doing well in math, but she did not know I was doing so poorly in every subject. [6]

While she slowly read my report card, reading everything one word at a time, I hurried into my room and started [7] to get ready for bed. A few minutes later, Mother came into my bedroom.

8   "Benjamin," she said, "are these your grades?" She held the card in front of me as if I hadn't seen it before.

9   "Oh, yeah, but you know, it doesn't mean much."

10   "No, that's not true, Bennie. It means a lot."

11   "Just a report card."

12   "But it's more than that."

13   Knowing I was in for it now, I prepared to listen, yet I was not all that interested. I did not like school very much and there was no reason why I should. Inasmuch as° I was the dumbest kid in the class, what did I have to look forward to? The others laughed at me and made jokes about me every day.

14   "Education is the only way you're ever going to escape poverty," she said. "It's the only way you're ever going to get ahead in life and be successful. Do you understand that?"

15   "Yes, Mother," I mumbled.

16   "If you keep on getting these kinds of grades you're going to spend the rest of your life on skid row, or at best sweeping floors in a factory. That's not the kind of life that I want for you. That's not the kind of life that God wants for you."

17   I hung my head, genuinely ashamed. My mother had been raising me and my older brother, Curtis, by herself. Having only a third-grade education herself, she knew the value of what she did not have. Daily she drummed into Curtis and me that we had to do our best in school.

18   "You're just not living up to your potential," she said. "I've got two mighty smart boys and I know they can do better."

19   I had done my best—at least I had when I first started at Higgins Elementary School. How could I do much when I did not understand anything going on in our class?

20   In Boston we had attended a parochial school, but I hadn't learned much because of a teacher who seemed more interested in talking to another female teacher than in teaching us. Possibly, this teacher was not solely to blame—perhaps I wasn't emotionally able to learn much. My parents had separated just before we went to Boston, when I was eight years old. I loved both my mother and father and went through considerable trauma° over their separating. For months afterward, I kept thinking that my parents would get back together, that my daddy would come home again the way he used to, and that we could be the same old family again—but he never came back. Consequently°, we moved to Boston and lived with Aunt Jean and Uncle William Avery in a tenement building for two years until Mother had saved enough money to bring us back to Detroit.

21   Mother kept shaking the report card at me as she sat on the side of my bed. "You have to work harder. You have to use that good brain that God gave you, Bennie. Do you understand that?"

22   "Yes, Mother." Each time she paused, I would dutifully say those words.

23   "I work among rich people, people who are educated," she said. "I watch how they act, and I know they can do anything they want to do. And so can you." She put her arm on my shoulder. "Bennie, you can do anything they can do—only you can do it better!"

24   Mother had said those words before. Often. At the time, they did not mean much to me. Why should they? I really believed that I was the dumbest kid in fifth grade, but of course, I never told her that.

25   "I just don't know what to do about you boys," she said. "I'm going to talk to God about you and Curtis." She paused, stared into space, then said (more to herself than to me), "I need the Lord's guid-

ance on what to do. You just can't bring in any more report cards like this."

26   As far as I was concerned, the report card matter was over.

27   The next day was like the previous ones—just another bad day in school, another day of being laughed at because I did not get a single problem right in arithmetic and couldn't get any words right on the spelling test. As soon as I came home from school, I changed into play clothes and ran outside. Most of the boys my age played softball, or the game I liked best, "Tip the Top."

28   We played Tip the Top by placing a bottle cap on one of the sidewalk cracks. Then taking a ball—any kind that bounced—we'd stand on a line and take turns throwing the ball at the bottle top, trying to flip it over. Whoever succeeded got two points. If anyone actually moved the cap more than a few inches, he won

five points. Ten points came if he flipped it into the air and it landed on the other side.

29   When it grew dark or we got tired, Curtis and I would finally go inside and watch TV. The set stayed on until we went to bed. Because Mother worked long hours, she was never home until just before we went to bed. Sometimes I would awaken when I heard her unlocking the door.

30   Two evenings after the incident with the report card, Mother came home about an hour before our bedtime. Curtis and I were sprawled out, watching TV. She walked across the room, snapped off the set, and faced both of us. "Boys," she said, "you're wasting too much of your time in front of that television. You don't get an education from staring at television all the time."

31   Before either of us could make a protest, she told us that she had been praying for wisdom. "The Lord's told me what to do," she said. "So from now on, you will not watch television, except for two preselected programs each week."

32   "Just *two* programs?" I could hardly believe she would say such a terrible thing. "That's not—"

33   "And *only* after you've done your homework. Furthermore, you don't play outside after school, either, until you've done all your homework."

34   "Everybody else plays outside right after school," I said, unable to think of anything except how bad it would be if I couldn't play with my friends. "I won't have any friends if I stay in the house all the time—"

35   "That may be," Mother said, "but everybody else is not going to be as successful as you are—"

36   "But, Mother—"

37   "This is what we're going to do. I asked God for wisdom, and this is the answer I got."

38 I tried to offer several other arguments, but Mother was firm. I glanced at Curtis, expecting him to speak up, but he did not say anything. He lay on the floor, staring at his feet.

39 "Don't worry about everybody else. The whole world is full of 'everybody else,' you know that? But only a few make a significant achievement."

40 The loss of TV and play time was bad enough. I got up off the floor, feeling as if everything was against me. Mother wasn't going to let me play with my friends, and there would be no more television—almost none, anyway. She was stopping me from having any fun in life.

41 "And that isn't all," she said. "Come back, Bennie."

42 I turned around, wondering what else there could be.

43 "In addition," she said, "to doing your homework, you have to read two books from the library each week. Every single week."

44 "Two books? Two?" Even though I was in fifth grade, I had never read a whole book in my life.

45 "Yes, two. When you finish reading them, you must write me a book report just like you do at school. You're not living up to your potential, so I'm going to see that you do."

46 Usually Curtis, who was two years older, was the more rebellious°. But this time he seemed to grasp the wisdom of what Mother said. He did not say one word.

47 She stared at Curtis. "You understand?"

48 He nodded.

49 "Bennie, is it clear?"

50 "Yes, Mother." I agreed to do what Mother told me—it wouldn't have occurred to me not to obey—but I did not like it. Mother was being unfair and demanding more of us than other parents did.

51 The following day was Thursday. After school, Curtis and I walked to the local branch of the library. I did not like it much, but then I had not spent that much time in any library.

52 We both wandered around a little in the children's section, not having any idea about how to select books or which books we wanted to check out.

Dr. Carson consults with physicians' assistant Carol James.

53 The librarian came over to us and asked if she could help. We explained that both of us wanted to check out two books.

54 "What kind of books would you like to read?" the librarian asked.

55 "Animals," I said after thinking about it. "Something about animals."

56 "I'm sure we have several that you'd like." She led me over to a section of books. She left me and guided Curtis to another section of the room. I flipped through the row of books until I found two that looked easy enough for me to read. One of them, *Chip, the Dam Builder*—about a beaver—was the first one I had

ever checked out. As soon as I got home, I started to read it. It was the first book I ever read all the way through even though it took me two nights. Reluctantly I admitted afterward to Mother that I really had liked reading about Chip.

57   Within a month I could find my way around the children's section like someone who had gone there all his life. By then the library staff knew Curtis and me and the kind of books we chose. They often made suggestions. "Here's a delightful book about a squirrel," I remember one of them telling me.

58   As she told me part of the story, I tried to appear indifferent, but as soon as she handed it to me, I opened the book and started to read.

59   Best of all, we became favorites of the librarians. When new books came in that they thought either of us would enjoy, they held them for us. Soon I became fascinated as I realized that the library had so many books—and about so many different subjects.

60   After the book about the beaver, I chose others about animals—all types of animals. I read every animal story I could get my hands on. I read books about wolves, wild dogs, several about squirrels, and a variety of animals that lived in other countries. Once I had gone through the animal books, I started reading about plants, then minerals, and finally rocks.

61   My reading books about rocks was the first time the information ever became practical to me. We lived near the railroad tracks, and when Curtis and I took the route to school that crossed by the tracks, I began paying attention to the crushed rock that I noticed between the ties.

62   As I continued to read more about rocks, I would walk along the tracks, searching for different kinds of stones, and then see if I could identify them.

63   Often I would take a book with me to make sure that I had labeled each stone correctly.

64   "Agate," I said as I threw the stone. Curtis got tired of my picking up stones and identifying them, but I did not care because I kept finding new stones all the time. Soon it became my favorite game to walk along the tracks and identify the varieties of stones. Although I did not realize it, within a very short period of time, I was actually becoming an expert on rocks.

65   Two things happened in the second half of fifth grade that convinced me of the importance of reading books.

66   First, our teacher, Mrs. Williamson, had a spelling bee every Friday afternoon. We'd go through all the words we'd had so far that year. Sometimes she also called out words that we were supposed to have learned in fourth grade. Without fail, I always went down on the first word.

67   One Friday, though, Bobby Farmer, whom everyone acknowledged as the smartest kid in our class, had to spell "agriculture" as his final word. As soon as the teacher pronounced his word, I thought, *I can spell that word.* Just the day before, I had learned it from reading one of my library books. I spelled it under my breath, and it was just the way Bobby spelled it.

68   *If I can spell "agriculture," I'll bet I can learn to spell any other word in the world. I'll bet I can learn to spell better than Bobby Farmer.*

69   Just that single word, "agriculture," was enough to give me hope.

70   The following week, a second thing happened that forever changed my life. When Mr. Jaeck, the science teacher, was teaching us about volcanoes, he held up an object that looked like a piece of black, glass-like rock. "Does anybody know

what this is? What does it have to do with volcanoes?"

71   Immediately, because of my reading, I recognized the stone. I waited, but none of my classmates raised their hands. I thought, *This is strange. Not even the smart kids are raising their hands.* I raised my hand.

72   "Yes, Benjamin," he said.

73   I heard laughter around me. The other kids probably thought it was a joke, or that I was going to say something stupid.

74   "Obsidian," I said.

75   "That's right!" He tried not to look startled, but it was obvious he hadn't expected me to give the correct answer.

76   "That's obsidian," I said, "and it's formed by the supercooling of lava when it hits the water." Once I had their attention and realized I knew information no other student had learned, I began to tell them everything I knew about the subject of obsidian, lava, lava flow, super-cooling, and compacting of the elements.

77   When I finally paused, a voice behind me whispered, "Is that Bennie Carson?"

78   "You're absolutely correct," Mr. Jaeck said and he smiled at me. If he had announced that I'd won a million-dollar lottery, I couldn't have been more pleased and excited.

79   "Benjamin, that's absolutely, absolutely right," he repeated with enthusiasm in his voice. He turned to the others and said, "That is wonderful! Class, this is a tremendous piece of information Benjamin has just given us. I'm very proud to hear him say this."

80   For a few moments, I tasted the thrill of achievement. I recall thinking, *Wow, look at them. They're all looking at me with admiration. Me, the dummy! The one everybody thinks is stupid. They're looking at me to see if this is really me speaking.*

81   Maybe, though, it was I who was the most astonished° one in the class. Although I had been reading two books a week because Mother told me to, I had not realized how much knowledge I was accumulating. True, I had learned to enjoy reading, but until then I hadn't realized how it connected with my school-work. That day—for the first time—I realized that Mother had been right. Reading is the way out of ignorance, and the road to achievement. I did not have to be the class dummy anymore.

82   For the next few days, I felt like a hero at school. The jokes about me stopped. The kids started to listen to me. *I'm starting to have fun with this stuff.*

83   As my grades improved in every subject, I asked myself, "Ben, is there any reason you can't be the smartest kid in the class? If you can learn about obsidian, you can learn about social studies and geography and math and science and everything."

84   That single moment of triumph pushed me to want to read more. From then on, it was as though I could not read enough books. Whenever anyone looked for me after school, they could usually find me in my bedroom—curled up, reading a library book—for a long time, the only thing I wanted to do. I had stopped caring about the TV programs I was missing; I no longer cared about playing Tip the Top or baseball anymore. I just wanted to read.

85   In a year and a half—by the middle of sixth grade—I had moved to the top of the class.

Vocabulary Check

1. In which sentence would the word **trauma** make sense?
   a. I love the _____ of a good comedy.
   b. The kidnapping of a child causes great _____ to parents.
   c. The _____ of spring makes Dad eager to get back to his gardening.

2. In which sentence would the word **astonished** make sense?
   a. My sister _____ me to a new flavor of ice cream.
   b. I accidentally unplugged the freezer and _____ a lot of food.
   c. We were _____ when our grandmother got engaged.

3. In the sentences below, the word **potential** means
   a. ability to progress.
   b. desire to play.
   c. physical strength.

   "You're just not living up to your potential," she said. "I've got two mighty smart boys and I know they can do better." (Paragraph 18)

Dr. Carson and his wife, Candy, are photographed at home with their sons (from left to right), Murray, B.J., and Rhoeyce.

4. In the sentences below, the word **dutifully** means
   a. obediently.
   b. laughingly.
   c. angrily.

   "'Yes, Mother.' Each time she paused, I would dutifully say those words." (Paragraph 22)

5. In the sentence below, the word **indifferent** means
   a. embarrassed.
   b. handsome.
   c. not interested.

   "As she told me part of the story, I tried to appear indifferent, but as soon as she handed it to me, I opened the book and started to read." (Paragraph 58)

SCORE: **(Number correct)** _____ **x 20 =** _____ **%**

Reading Check

Central Point and Main Ideas

1. What is the central point of the reading?
   a. Ben discovered he loved reading about animals, plants, minerals, and rocks.
   b. In his new school, Ben was at first considered the dumbest kid in class.
   c. Turning off the TV and reading books helped Ben become a great student.

2. What is the main idea of paragraph 4?
   a. Ben came to believe he was really stupid.
   b. Ben learned to be very funny in school.
   c. Ben's mother did not know what was happening in class.

3. What is the main idea of paragraph 81?
   a. Ben no longer cared what anybody in class thought of him.
   b. Ben had been reading two books a week because his mother told him to.
   c. Ben finally realized that through reading, he could succeed in school.

Supporting Details

4. Ben's mother had
   a. finished third grade.
   b. finished junior high.
   c. attended college.

5. Ben's mother asked Ben and Curtis to
   a. watch no TV at all.
   b. write book reports for her.
   c. finish their homework at school every day.

6. When Curtis heard his mother's new rules about TV and reading,
   a. he shouted angrily at her.
   b. he left the house.
   c. he accepted them quietly.

7. Ben surprised his science teacher by knowing a lot about
   a. volcanic rock.
   b. how beavers build dams.
   c. agriculture.

Conclusions

8. You can conclude from paragraph 79 that
   a. Ben knew more about volcanic rock than Mr. Jaeck did.
   b. Ben was embarrassed by Mr. Jaeck's praise.
   c. Mr. Jaeck wanted to encourage Ben to keep reading and learning.

9. You can conclude from paragraph 83 that
    a. Ben's favorite subject was rocks.
    b. success gave Ben confidence.
    c. Ben disliked math and science.

10. You can conclude from paragraph 84 that
    a. even though he read a lot, Ben was still a slow reader.
    b. the library soon ran out of books for Ben to read.
    c. being smart and successful brought Ben more pleasure than watching TV and playing did.

SCORE: **(Number correct)** _____ **x 10 =** _____ **%**

Questions for Thinking and Discussion

1. Ben once thought of himself as "the dumbest kid in class." How did he form this opinion of himself? How do you think it affected the way he did school work?

2. Why did Ben's mother limit her sons to watching two TV programs per week? How would you react if your TV viewing were limited? Do you agree that too much TV can be bad for children?

3. Ben's mother told him, "Education is the only way you're ever going to escape poverty." How could education help him escape poverty?

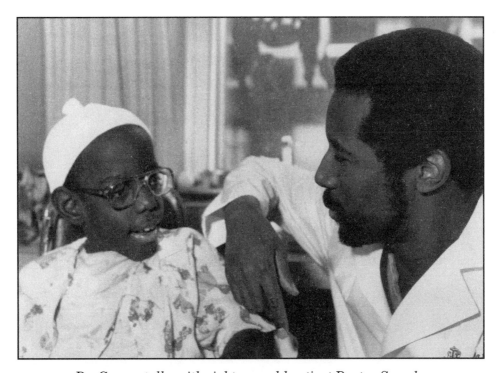

Dr. Carson talks with eight-year-old patient Dontae Sample.

Dr. Carson finds time between surgical operations to deliver motivational talks to groups of schoolchildren.

Ideas for Writing

1. Ben's self-confidence got a big boost when he correctly answered a question in class that no one else could answer. Write a paper about a time you were successful at something. Describe what you did, how others reacted, and how you felt.

2. Ben describes a bad experience with his teacher in Boston and a good experience with his science teacher in Detroit. Think of a teacher who was especially helpful or unhelpful to you. Write a paper titled either "A Helpful Teacher" or "A Teacher Who Was Not Helpful." Describe what the teacher did and how you were affected.

20 / Juanita Lira

Words to Watch

resents (5): feels angry about
My friend *resents* being treated like a two-year-old by his boss.

inferior (6): low in quality or value
Our old car may be *inferior*, but it gets us where we want to go.

fulfill (8): bring to life; make happen
My mother is about to *fulfill* her dream of visiting a brother she hasn't seen in twenty years.

extraordinary (9): very unusual; amazing
The girl made the *extraordinary* claim that she had seen a ghost at school.

campaign (25): planned effort to accomplish a goal
I began a *campaign* to get my brother to quit smoking.

Juanita Lira stands in front of the house where she lived as a child.

Many years have passed since Juanita Lira attended elementary and middle school, but she cannot forget her experiences there. 1

Juanita grew up in Azteca, the poorest neighborhood of Laredo, Texas. Her father was a hard-working barber. Her mother stayed home in the traditional Mexican way, caring for the house and for Juanita and her brother. Azteca was a neighborhood of small wooden shacks set only inches back from the dirt street. There were no yards around the houses or parks to play in. The families of Azteca had outhouses instead of indoor toilets. 2

Juanita's parents were protective of their only daughter. They did not want her crossing town to attend Laredo's public school. Instead, they scraped together the money to send her to the nearby Catholic school. The tuition was seven dollars a month, a lot of money for the family. 3

Like many of the children of Laredo, a town near the Mexican border, Juanita arrived at first grade speaking no English. But she was filled with the desire to learn. "My parents put great value on education," she says today. "They believed it was the way out of poverty." Juanita's earliest memory is of her grandmother carrying her in her arms, singing these words: *"M'hijita, vas hacer maestra"*—You will be a teacher, little girl. By the time Juanita was 7, she 4

177

was tutoring younger neighborhood children in exchange for cans of soda.

5   Juanita knew she would need to learn English in school. But in looking back on her elementary-school years, she resents° her teachers' methods. "The nuns spoke no Spanish," she says. "They made us feel that our language was no good. We were actually fined for speaking Spanish, even on the playground! Imagine a bunch of little first graders playing with friends—of course we used the language we knew. And the nuns would follow us around and say, 'That will be ten cents for speaking Spanish.'"

6   Juanita and the other children were made to feel their language was second-class. For that reason, Juanita remembers, "We began to wonder if our parents were also second-class since they didn't know English." In addition, some children were made to feel inferior° for being poor. "The teachers would have fundraisers for the school, and they'd ask who could donate a cake to be raffled off." For most of the families of Azteca, a cake was an unheard-of luxury. But a few of the better-off students could provide one. "So those kids with more money became the teachers' favorites," says Juanita. "They were chosen to go the blackboard, to lead activities, to do special chores."

7   The situation became even worse in seventh grade when Juanita's class was divided in two. One group was enrolled in college-preparatory classes. The other—Juanita's group—was assigned to business courses. The division was made without any discussion with the students or their parents. "There is nothing wrong with being a business student," Juanita declares. "A lot of good students take business courses. But in our school, business students were regarded as the 'dummy group.'" Juanita remembers the anger she felt when the college-prep group put on a play. Her business group

was not invited to join but served as the audience. "I must have still known that I had some ability," Juanita recalls. "It seemed terribly unfair to me that I couldn't have opportunities like the college-prep group."

8   Unlike Juanita, many of her classmates accepted their teachers' views of them and did poorly. A number dropped out before graduating. "When children are told they are dumb and worthless, they fulfill° that prediction," says Juanita. Even Juanita was only an average student.

9   But then something extraordinary° happened. One of the school's twelve teachers, a nun named Sister Goretti, approached Juanita. She suggested that Juanita run for the office of student council secretary.

10   "I was absolutely speechless," Juanita recalls. "Student council was 'it.' Only jocks and cheerleaders got into student council. You weren't allowed to run unless a nun nominated you." Sister Goretti nominated Juanita.

11   Juanita didn't expect to win. There were two slates of candidates. One was made up of popular kids. The candidate for secretary on that slate was a cheerleader, an Anglo girl. "And then there was me—Juanita Who?" she remembers with a laugh. But when the candidates were required to give speeches in front of the student body, Juanita became enthusiastic. "I really got into that speech," she says. "Finally, there was a spark! Someone had noticed me and thought I could do well! I gave my speech, and I felt really good about it. And I guess I had more friends than I thought because I was the only candidate on my slate to win."

12   The next year, Juanita ran for student council vice president and won. "Student council really brought me out of my shell," she says. "It gave me the confidence to try to reach other goals."

13   So after high school, Juanita enrolled in a junior college. At first, she took secretarial courses, but gradually, she renewed her old desire to be a teacher. Choir scholarships and a National Defense Loan allowed her to transfer from junior college and to Texas A & I University in Kingsville. She earned her bachelor's degree in education there.

14   With her teaching degree in hand, Juanita decided to return to Laredo. She wanted to teach the kind of poor, Spanish-speaking children she and her classmates had been.

15   She got more than she bargained for. Her school was in a neighborhood called Santa Niño. It was nearly as poor as Azteca. Her third-grade class contained forty-one children. They ranged in age from 8 to 13. Many children were from migrant worker families. They had been held back in school because their constant traveling had made it impossible for them to receive the steady schooling needed to move ahead.

16   Effectively teaching forty-one students with a five-year age span was a nearly impossible task. But Juanita tackled the job with enthusiasm. She broke the class into several reading groups and spent part of the school day working with each. "But 8 to 13! Can you imagine!" she says. "I'd read a story like 'The Little Red Hen' and when I'd get to the part that says, 'Not I, said the duck,' the eight-year-olds would quack, and the thirteen-year-olds would roll their eyes."

17   As Juanita dealt with her students, she learned about dealing with their parents, too. One older student, José Luis, was giving her a lot of trouble. Thirteen years old and bigger than his young teacher, he was loud and disrespectful. His parents did not have a telephone, so she sent a message home with José's sister, asking their father to come to school.

18   The next day during class, the door opened, and a man walked in. "He was a big, tough-looking guy, and he said, 'I'm José Luis's father. What's the problem?' I tried to get him to step out in the hallway, but he insisted on talking right there. Finally I said, 'Well, he's rude.' The father proceeded to bawl out José Luis in front of the entire class. He then finished with a promise that he would come back and whip José Luis with a belt if he continued to misbehave." Juanita both shakes her head and laughs a little at that memory. "José Luis was an *angel* after that day, but I didn't feel good about his being humiliated in front of the class," she says. "After that, I was always careful to tell parents I wanted to see them *after* school, not in the middle of it!"

19   Juanita and her husband, Juan, also an elementary teacher, taught for several more years. Then the couple decided to

begin work on their doctoral degrees at the University of Texas in Austin. Juanita then went on to an administrative job as vice-principal of a school of eight hundred eighth-graders. She was in charge of discipline.

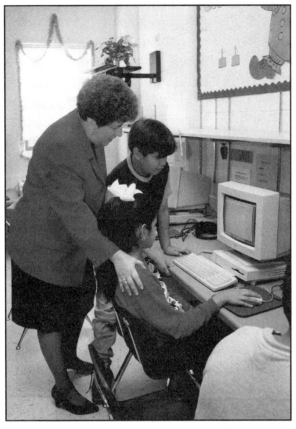

Juanita visits with students in the computer lab at one of the elementary schools she oversees.

20   "My friends thought I had lost my mind," she says. "But I had this conviction that as vice-principal, I could do positive things for the students."

21   One of Juanita's strategies was to get the troublemakers onto her team. "I invited them in before any problems started," she says. "I explained to them that I knew they were leaders and that I needed their help. I didn't want any fighting because I cared about them and didn't want them to be hurt."

22   Her plan worked. The students warned her of upcoming fights. They let her know when students were carrying weapons to school. By the end of the year, Juanita had thirty knives locked in a drawer in her office.

23   Although she was the person in charge of discipline, Juanita often felt more like a counselor. "I listened and listened and listened," she says. "Eighth grade is a fascinating, tough time of life. Everything is changing so fast for these kids, and they need people to talk to. I learned a lot in that one year, and I was looking forward to coming back."

24   Instead, Juanita accepted an invitation to become principal of an elementary school in Laredo. The school, she discovered, was in terrible shape. "The students had rock-bottom test scores," she explains. "The building was disorderly. Students spent their class time cutting out paper flowers for floats, watching videos, or having cheerleading practice. Parents and teachers wouldn't go to the principal's office because the only reason anyone ever went there was to get yelled at."

25   Juanita swung into action. First, she and her assistant principal began a campaign° to raise the teachers' self-esteem. "We'd put notes in their mailboxes complimenting them on good things they'd done. I encouraged them to come into the office just to chat and let me know how things were going. They began to take more pride in their work. Along with the students, they got excited when our school eventually competed in and won science fairs and talent contests."

26   Then Juanita increased parents' participation. "You've got to get parents involved in the schools," she insists. "They are their children's first teachers. When the children see their parents' interest in school, they do better. We teachers cannot do it alone."

27   How did she encourage parents to get involved? Juanita remembered how

unwelcome her own mother and father had felt visiting her school when she was a child. What would have made them feel welcome in her elementary school? She had some ideas, and she put them into practice.

28   "We conducted our meetings in Spanish and provided child care for the little ones," she explains. "We'd have parenting sessions on things like how to help your child with homework. The kids and parents would come in together to the library to choose books to read to one another. We had activities for the grandparents. And we'd always have food—the key to success! We'd serve tamales and other things the parents were comfortable with. We did everything we could think of to make coming to school a happy, welcoming thing, not threatening. We told them in every way we could, 'We're all in this together.'"

29   By the end of Juanita's first year as principal, the school's test scores had risen 28 percent. When she had been there four years, the school was regularly receiving awards for excellence. "It's a wonderful school today," she says proudly. "We've got great teachers, great kids."

30   Because of her success as a principal, Juanita was asked to become director of elementary education for the United Independent School District of Laredo. In that position today, she oversees sixteen elementary schools. She is helping those schools achieve the same kind of success she had inspired in the school where she had been principal.

31   And she never loses sight of her primary goal—to make sure the students of Laredo are encouraged to learn and to grow, one child at a time. "It's possible to work on your own self-esteem," she adds. "You can tell yourself, 'I can do this.' But it helps a lot to have someone else telling you the same thing. And that's what I can do. I can say to children, with all my heart, 'I believe in you.'"

Juanita meets with principals and staff members in her elementary school district.

Vocabulary Check

1. In which sentence would the word **inferior** make sense?
   a. Our gym teacher makes the poor athletes in class feel _____.
   b. The more you practice piano, the more _____ you will become.
   c. I was _____ when I was unfairly accused of copying another student's paper.

2. In which sentence would the word **campaign** make sense?
   a. My cousin went to a Girl Scout _____ for a week last summer.
   b. It is every citizen's _____ to vote.
   c. The _____ to clean up the school grounds was very successful.

3. In the sentences below, the word **slates** means
   a. lists.
   b. names.
   c. dates.

   "There were two slates of candidates. One was made up of popular kids." (Paragraph 11)

4. In the sentences below, the word **conviction** means
   a. fear.
   b. belief.
   c. memory.

   "'My friends thought I had lost my mind,' she says. 'But I had this conviction that as vice-principal, I could do positive things for the students.'" (Paragraph 20)

Standing with Juanita is her husband, Dr. Juan Lira, who is also an educator.

5. In the sentence below, the word **strategies** means
   a. problems.
   b. accidents.
   c. methods.

   "One of Juanita's strategies was to get the troublemakers onto her team." (Paragraph 21)

SCORE: (Number correct) _____ x 20 = _____%

Reading Check

Central Point and Main Ideas

1. What is the central point of the reading?
   a. Teachers should not make students feel ashamed of their native languages.
   b. With the help of one teacher's attention, Juanita gained the confidence to set goals for herself and to help others aim high.
   c. Under Juanita's leadership, a school with "rock-bottom test scores" became an outstanding school.

2. What is the main idea of paragraph 7?
   a. Part of Juanita's seventh-grade class was assigned to college-preparatory classes.
   b. Part of Juanita's seventh-grade class was assigned to business classes.
   c. Juanita's seventh-grade class was unfairly divided into college-prep and business groups.

3. What is the main idea of paragraph 28?
   a. It's important to serve food at meetings if you want lots of people to come.
   b. Kids and parents came together to the library to pick out books.
   c. Juanita made sure that parents felt comfortable visiting her school.

Supporting Details

4. Juanita's parents sent her to a Catholic school because
   a. the public school had a poor reputation.
   b. Juanita had a scholarship to attend the Catholic school.
   c. the Catholic school was closer to their home.

5. Sister Goretti suggested that
   a. Juanita should run for student council secretary.
   b. Juanita should plan to attend college.
   c. Juanita should drop out of school and get married.

6. As vice-principal of a large eighth-grade school, Juanita was in charge of
   a. teacher education.
   b. student discipline.
   c. bilingual programs.

Conclusions

7. You can conclude from paragraph 5 that
   a. by fining the children for speaking Spanish, the nuns were able to raise a great amount of money for the church.
   b. the nuns did not want first graders to play on the playground.
   c. Juanita and her classmates began to feel ashamed of their language.

8. You can conclude from paragraph 7 that
   a. Juanita's group was not considered smart enough to be in the play.
   b. Juanita wanted to be in the business group.
   c. The play that the college-prep group put on was poorly done.

9. You can conclude from paragraph 24 that
   a. there was only one elementary school in Laredo.
   b. before Juanita came to the school, students had spent a lot of time on academics.
   c. the previous principal had not done a very good job.

10. You can conclude from paragraph 29 that
    a. the students in Juanita's school were smarter than the ones who had been there with the previous principal.
    b. Juanita had hired better teachers.
    c. Juanita's methods of inspiring teachers and students had succeeded.

SCORE: **(Number correct)** _____ x 10 = _____%

Questions for Thinking and Discussion

1. Do you believe, as Juanita does, that the way her seventh-grade class was divided in two groups was unfair ? Explain.

2. Juanita says, "When children are told they are dumb and worthless, they fulfill that prediction." What does she mean by this statement? Explain why you do or do not agree with her.

3. When Juanita became vice principal, she decided to try to "get the troublemakers onto her team." Why do you think the "troublemakers" cooperated instead of making trouble?

Ideas for Writing

1. When Juanita became principal of a troubled school, she made many changes. What changes do you think would improve a school where you have been a student? Write a paper describing two or three changes you would make, and tell why you would make each change.

2. Juanita found it very hard to teach a class with a wide range of ages. Have you ever had to do something that seemed very difficult? Write a paper telling the story of a time that you had trouble with something but kept trying. Explain also how you succeeded in the end or how you are determined to continue until you do succeed.